The Practical Ventriloquist

Anonymous

Alpha Editions

This edition published in 2024

ISBN 9789361473845

Design and Setting By

Alpha Editions

www.alphaedis.com

Email - info@alphaedis.com

As per information held with us this book is in Public Domain.
This book is a reproduction of an important historical work.
Alpha Editions uses the best technology to reproduce historical work
in the same manner it was first published to preserve its original nature.
Any marks or number seen are left intentionally to preserve.

Contents

CHAPTER I INTRODUCTORY. — - 1 -

CHAPTER II. OF PALMISTRY AND PASSES. — - 4 -

FIRST TRICK.—To command a dime to pass into the centre of a ball of Berlin wool, so that it will not be discovered till the ball is unwound to the very last of its threads. — - 7 -

SECOND TRICK.—To change a bowl of ink into clear water, with gold fish in it. — - 9 -

THIRD TRICK.—The Dancing Egg. — - 10 -

FOURTH TRICK.—The Walking Cent. — - 11 -

CHAPTER III. TRICKS WITH AND WITHOUT COLLUSION. — - 14 -

TRICK 5.—To make a quarter and a penny change places, while held in the hands of two spectators. — - 17 -

TRICK 6.—Another trick with the dime, handkerchief, and an orange or lemon. — - 17 -

TRICK 7.—How to double your pocket money. — - 18 -

TRICK 8.—The injured handkerchief restored. — - 19 -

TRICK 9.—To make a large die pass through the crown of a hat without injuring it. — - 20 -

TRICK 10.—To produce from a silk handkerchief bon-bons, candies, nuts, etc. — - 21 -

CHAPTER IV. PRACTICE. — - 23 -

TRICK 11.—A sudden and unexpected supply of feathers from under a silk handkerchief or cloth. — - 24 -

TRICK 12.—Heads or Tails? — - 26 -

TRICK 13.—To cook pancakes or a flat plum cake in a hat, over some candles. — - 27 -

TRICK 14.—TO EAT A DISH OF PAPER SHAVINGS, AND DRAW THEM OUT OF YOUR MOUTH LIKE AN ATLANTIC CABLE. - 29 -

TRICK 15.—How to cut off a nose—of course without actual injury. - 30 -

CHAPTER V. TRICKS BY MAGNETISM, CHEMISTRY, GALVANISM, OR ELECTRICITY. - 32 -

TRICK 16.—The watch obedient to the word of command. - 33 -

TRICK 17. - 35 -

TRICK 18.—A chemical trick to follow one where a young friend has assisted. - 35 -

TRICK 19.—To draw three spools off two tapes without those spools having to come off the ends of the tapes, and while the four ends of the tapes are held by four persons. - 36 -

TRICK 20.—To restore a tape whole after it has been cut in the middle. - 38 -

CHAPTER VI. ON THE CONTINUITY OF TRICKS. - 43 -

TRICK 21.—The invisible hen: a very useful trick for supplying eggs for breakfast or dinner. - 46 -

A SERIES OF TRICKS, 22, 23, 24.—The chief agent being a plain gold ring. - 49 -

TRICK 22. - 49 -

TRICK 23. - 50 -

TRICK 24. - 50 -

CHAPTER VII. FRIENDLY SUGGESTIONS. - 52 -

TRICK 25.—The Conjuror's "Bonus Genius," or Familiar Messenger. - 53 -

TRICK 26.—The Shower of Money. - 55 -

TRICK 27.—To Furnish Ladies With a Magic Supply of Tea or Coffee, at their selection, From One and the Same Jug. - 56 -

TRICK 28.—A Pleasing Exhibition for both the Performer and the Audience to view when they feel a little Exhausted.	- 57 -
TRICK 29.—To Furnish a Treat to the Gentlemen.	- 58 -
VENTRILOQUISM MADE EASY.	- 60 -
WHAT IS VENTRILOQUISM?	- 60 -
VENTRILOQUISM AMONGST THE ANCIENTS.	- 63 -
MODERN PROFESSORS OF THE ART.	- 64 -
THE THEORY OF VENTRILOQUISM.	- 68 -
THE MEANS BY WHICH IT IS EFFECTED.	- 72 -
PRACTICAL ILLUSTRATIONS.	- 73 -
POLYPHONIC IMITATIONS.	- 80 -
A MOUNTAIN ECHO.	- 81 -
POINTS TO BE REMEMBERED.	- 82 -
CONCLUDING REMARKS.	- 83 -
THE MAGIC WHISTLE.	- 84 -

CHAPTER I
INTRODUCTORY.

My object in writing these hints on CONJURING is for the benefit of amateurs to promote lively and entertaining amusement for the home circle and social gatherings.

My large experience enables me to explain and simplify many of the best tricks and illusions of the art. I present the key to many of the mystical mysteries which have puzzled and bewildered our childhood days as well as confounded us in our maturer years.

The young student can in a very short time, if he be in the least of an ingenious turn, amuse and astonish his friends, neighbors and acquaintances.

Preference has been given to those tricks which suggest others, the more complete and difficult performances and illusions have been passed by as being out of place; I shall not, therefore, in these elementary papers advert to those experiments which require ample resources, or a prepared stage, for exhibiting them—or which can only be displayed to advantage by consummate skill and the most adroit manipulation—but confine my remarks at present to those branches of the art to the performance of which a young amateur may aspire with prospect of success.

A few hours' practice will enable the learner to execute the simple tricks that I shall first treat of; and they will only require for their display such articles as are readily available in every household. Most of them will be supplied by any company of a few friends, and if not in the parlor, can be brought from no greater distance than the kitchen or housekeeper's room; such as handkerchiefs, coins, oranges, or eggs, a glass bowl, etc., etc. There may only remain a few inexpensive articles to be supplied from repositories for the sale of conjuring apparatus, or they may be had direct from the publishers of this work.

It may be well explicitly to avow that the time is quite gone by when people will really believe that conjuring is to be done by supernatural agencies. No faith is now reposed in the "black art of sorcery," or even in the art to which the less repulsive name was given of "white magic." Many years have elapsed since conjurors have seriously assumed to themselves any credit as possessing supernatural powers, or as enabled by spiritual agency to reveal that which is unknown to science and philosophy, or mysteriously to work astonishing marvels.

A well-marked contrast exists between the old school of conjurors and those of modern times. The former, who used boldly to profess that they employed mysterious rites and preternatural agency, designedly put the spectator upon false interpretations, while they studiously avoided giving any elucidation of the phenomena, nor would ever admit that the wonders displayed were to be accounted for by the principles of science and natural philosophy.

Modern conjurors advance no such pretensions. They use as scientifically as possible the natural properties of matter to aid in their exhibition of wonderful results. They are content to let the exhibition of their art appear marvelous. They sometimes mystify the matter, and so increase the puzzle, in order to heighten the interest and amusement of the spectators; but they throw aside any solemn asseveration of possessing hidden powers, or of ability to fathom mysterious secrets.

It may be admitted that proficients and exhibitors still adopt language that has become current with conjurors, and in common parlance it may be asserted that the wonderful Mr. So-and-So undertakes to pass some solid object through a wall or a table; to change black into white, and white into black; to place rings in closely-fastened boxes, or draw money out of people's ears; and conjurors may with ridiculous humor distract the attention of spectators, so that accurate observation is not fixed upon the object that is to undergo before their eyes some singular transformation; but no outrageous bombast or positive falsehoods are commonly advanced. And the practical meaning of any exaggerated pretension is clearly understood to mean no more than that Mr. So-and-So undertakes to present before you what, TO ALL APPEARANCE, is the conversion of black into white, or vice versa; and the audience are clearly aware that no more is assumed to be presented to them than a very striking illusion, undistinguishable from a reality; and how this is effected will be in many cases wholly untraceable, and therefore the trick is inimitable.

We may be permitted to feel some pleasure in the conviction that the exhibition of our art in its more striking exploits is really marvelous, and very attractive; for we certainly have the power of placing some astonishing phenomena before our audience; and we may surely prize the estimation with which the uninitiated are disposed to honor us, but we erect no vain-glorious assumptions upon these data, as we are quite contented with fair praise intelligently accorded to us. And so far from closely concealing the principles and arcana of our science, we are ready plainly to avow that it all depends upon faculties that all may attain by patient culture, and exhibit by careful practice. Undoubtedly there are less and greater degrees of excellence to be obtained by proportionate intelligence and dexterity. There are attainments in the art, at which, by natural qualification and peculiar adaptation, special study, practice, and experience enable some few only to arrive. These qualifications cannot be easily communicated to every one who might wish to possess them; and therefore the highest adepts will ever have an incommunicable distinction. But this is no more than is the case in the medical, the legal, and any learned profession, in all which the most eminent proficients reserve to themselves, or unavoidably retain, an unquestioned superiority. At the same time there is much in our art that may be communicated, and the present papers will show to our friends that we are willing to impart to others such portions of our art as they are capable of acquiring; and we trust that what we shall communicate to them will furnish them much rational recreation among themselves, and enable them to supply innocent and interesting amusement to their friends and companions.

CHAPTER II.
OF PALMISTRY AND PASSES.

The true nature and limit of the art of Conjuring has now been defined—what it is that we assume to do, and wherein we have discontinued the exaggerated pretensions of the conjurors of the old school; and I have hinted in what respects, and within what bounds, a young amateur may gim at exhibiting some amusing experiments in our art. But it remains for me to explain the grand pre-requisite for a novice to cultivate before he should attempt to exhibit before others even the simplest tricks of prestidigitation or legerdemain, to which we at present confine our attention.

I have first to speak of PALMISTRY, not in the sense that the fortune-teller uses the word, but as expressing the art of the conjuror in secreting articles in the PALM of one hand while he appears to transfer those articles to his other hand. It is absolutely necessary that the young amateur should acquire the habit of doing this so adroitly as to escape the observation of others while doing it openly before their eyes.

The two principal passes are the following:

> FIRST PASS; or, method of apparently carrying an object from the right hand to the left, while actually retaining it in the right hand.

The reader will please to observe that the illustrative sketches depict the hands of the performer as seen by himself.

FIRST POSITION OF PASS 1.

The right hand, having the knuckles and back of the fingers turned toward the spectators, and holding openly a cent, or some similar object, between the thumb and forefinger, must be moved toward the left hand.

The left hand must be held out, with the back of the hand toward the ground, as exhibited in the illustration. (Fig. 1.)

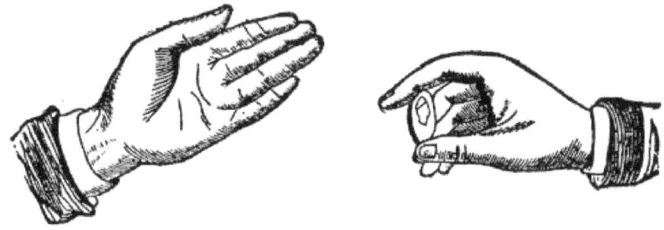

Fig. 1.
First Position of Pass 1.

SECOND POSITION OF PASS 1.

The left hand must appear to close over the object that is brought toward it, at the same instant that the right hand secretes and withdraws that object.

The left hand that appeared to receive it must continue closed. The right hand, though it actually retains the object, must be allowed to hang loosely over it, so that it appears to have nothing in it.

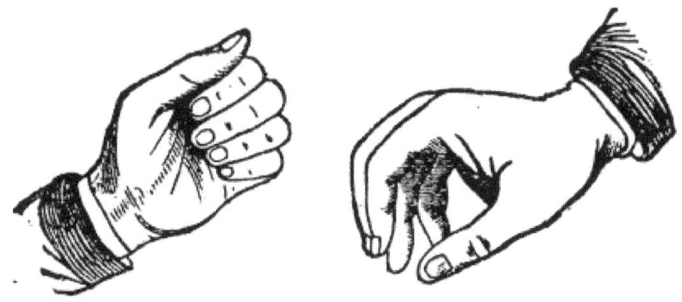

Fig. 2.
Second Position of Pass 1.

The performer then may blow upon the closed left hand, and may say, "Fly," or "Begone," or any similar expression, and then open his left hand, holding it forward. Of course there is nothing in it, and the object seems to have flown from it, and the spectators are much surprised.

> SECOND PASS.—Method of apparently transferring an object from the left hand to the right, while retaining it in the left hand.

FIRST POSITION.

Let the left hand hold up the object in its open palm. The right hand is brought toward the left hand, but only appears to grasp it.

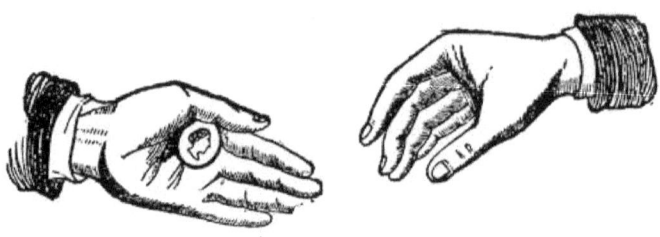

FIG. 3.
First Position of Pass 2.

SECOND POSITION.

The left hand secretes the object in its palm, while the fingers are allowed to fall loosely down, appearing to retain nothing under them. At the very same moment the right hand must be closed, and remain in shape as if containing the object, with the second joints of the fingers pointed toward the spectators, and the back of the hand toward the ground. The performer then holding his right hand forward, may blow on it and say "Change—fly," and opening that hand, the spectator deems the object has passed away from it, though in fact it has remained all along in the left hand.

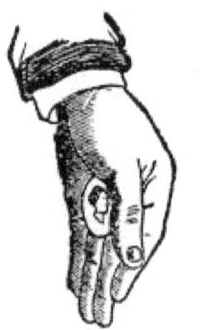 

FIG. 4.
Second Position of Pass 2.

The illusion in either of these passes is, that the spectator seeing both hands move as if the object were passing from one to the other, thinks it has done so; whereas, in fact, the object always remains in the hand where it was first visible to the spectators. The BACK of that hand where the object is first displayed must afterwards be kept well toward the spectators.

Observe, the eye of the performer must rest always on the hand or object at which he desires the spectators to look, and whatever he wishes them not to notice, he himself must refrain from looking at.

If it is not required that the very object that has been held up in these passes be seen again by the spectators, the performer must quietly pocket it, or drop it on a handkerchief on his table, or inside a hat, or otherwise get rid of it as soon as he conveniently can.

On the contrary, if that very object must be again produced or transferred to a person standing at some little distance, this must be effected by one of the following methods:

Either you must take care beforehand to place adroitly in that person's cap or pocket a double or similar object.

Or, you must walk up to him, and putting your hand on his hair, sleeve, or pocket, quickly place there the object you have all along retained, and which you must pretend by this manœuvre to find in his possession.

Or, lastly, you will see in the first trick subjoined, a method of substituting one object for another.

FIRST TRICK.—To command a dime to pass into the centre of a ball of Berlin wool, so that it will not be discovered till the ball is unwound to the very last of its threads.

REQUISITE PREPARATIONS, TO BE MADE PRIVATELY.

You will require a glass bowl or quart basin, and you must have a flattened tube of tin about four inches long. It must be just large enough to let a dime slide easily through it by its own weight. Round the end on this tube wind a ball of Berlin wool of bright color, covering about two inches of the tube, and projecting about an inch beyond the end of it. Place this ball with the tube in it in your right-hand pocket of coat tail, (or in the left breast-pocket, if that is large enough to hold it completely covered.) Lastly, place a dime concealed in the palm of your left hand.

Commence the exhibition of the trick by requesting one of the spectators to mark a dime (or cent) of his own, so that he will be sure to know it again. Then ask him to lend you that coin. Holding it up in your right hand, you may say, "Now, ladies and gentlemen, this is the marked dime which I shall experiment with. The gentleman has accurately marked it, so that there can be no mistake about its identity when reproduced." Then by Pass 1 pretend to transfer the marked coin to your left hand, but in reality retain it in your right hand. Next, hand with your left hand your own dime (which had been secreted in that hand) to some person, and request him to hold it. Choose for this person some one three or four yards distant from yourself, and also from the person who originally marked the coin. It is unnecessary to explain that you do so, lest the two should compare notes. Of course, the person who is asked to hold it will believe that it is the very dime that was borrowed.

You may proceed to say: "Now we want a ball of worsted." So, placing your right hand in your pocket, pretend to feel about for something in your pocket, and while doing so you must place the dime in the top of the tin tube, and shake it down. Then carefully draw the tube out of the ball of worsted; and leave the tube in your pocket, but draw the ball out of your pocket, pressing it together while doing so.

Then request some one to feel the ball in order to ascertain that it has no opening towards its centre.

You may here make some humorous remark about your having such a ball in your pocket. As for instance:

"Ladies may think it odd that I have such a ball of Berlin wool in my pocket. It was bought to please my cousin Mary Ann, or my Aunt Tabitha. Well, it will do very fairly for our experiment."

Then request some one to hold the glass basin containing the woollen ball. While you retain in your hand the end of the woollen thread, address the gentleman who has consented to hold the dime, asking him to hand it to you. Take it in your right hand, pretend by Pass 1 to transfer it to your left hand, but in reality keep it concealed in your right hand.

Holding up your closed left hand, (which in fact has nothing in it,) you may say:

"Now, dime, pass along this woollen thread into the very centre of the woollen ball which is there held in the glass bowl or basin."

Blow upon your left hand, and show that the dime is gone.

You must adroitly get rid of the dime, which has remained secreted in your right hand, by placing it in your pocket or sleeve while making some humorous remark, or while asking some lady or gentleman to draw the woollen thread till it is all unwound. It will be done the quicker by letting the ball be confined loosely in the bowl with two fingers preventing its leaping out.

Draw attention to how completely the coin is wrapped up till you arrive at the very last circles, when it will drop into the bowl.

Hand the dime to the owner who marked it, and let him declare whether he recognizes it as the very one he lent you. His affirmative will surprise the spectators.

SECOND TRICK.—To change a bowl of ink into clear water, with gold fish in it.

REQUISITE PREPARATION, TO BE MADE PRIVATELY BEFOREHAND.

The same glass bowl as in previous trick. If your bowl has not a foot to it, it must be placed on something that will hold it high above your table. Some small fish, a white plate or saucer, a piece of black silk just fitting the inside of your bowl, a spoon of peculiar construction, so that in a hollow handle it will retain about a teaspoonful of ink, which will not run out as long as a hole near the top of the handle is kept covered or stopped. A large tumbler and two or three minnows will do for a simpler exhibition, but will, of course, not be so pleasing to the eye.

Place the black silk so as to cover the part of the bowl that is shaded; when damp it will adhere to the glass. Pour in clear water to fill the space covered by the black silk, and place the fish in the water.

FIG. 5.

Commence the trick in public thus: Holding the spoon-handle slanting up and uncovering the hole in the handle, the ink which you have placed in the handle will run into the bowl of the spoon, and the spoon being held carefully to the surface of the water, concealing the black silk, will give the spectators the impression that you fill the spoon from the glass bowl.

Pour the spoonful of ink on a white saucer, and show it round to convince the spectators it is ink. They will see it is undeniably ink, and they will conclude, if the spoon were properly lifted out of the bowl, that the glass bowl contains nothing but ink.

Borrowing a silk handkerchief, place it for a few seconds over the bowl, and feigning to be inviting fish to come to the bowl, exclaim "Change!" Then, placing your hand on the edge of the bowl near yourself, draw off the handkerchief, and with it take care to catch hold also of the black silk. The bowl when uncovered will exhibit the fish swimming about in clear water. While the spectators are surprised at the fish, return the handkerchief, having first dropped out of it the black silk on your side of the table. Decline giving any explanation, as people will not thank you for dispelling the illusion.

THIRD TRICK.—The Dancing Egg.

REQUISITE PREPARATION TO BE MADE IN PRIVATE.

An egg-shell that has been blown (my young friends will know that the way to blow an egg is to make a small hole at each end of the egg. Then, by blowing at one end, the yolk will be driven out, and the egg-shell be left empty.)

Make a hole also on the side of the egg, in which insert a chip of wood, or a small pin, held by a fine black silk thread, about twelve or fourteen inches long, which must have a loop at the far end, which loop fasten to a button on the coat or waistcoat; and have on a dark vest, otherwise the dark thread becoming visible, will reveal the moving power.

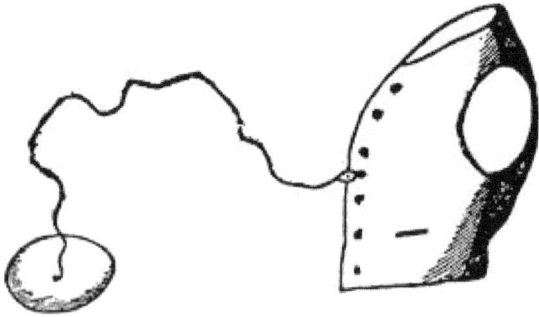

FIG. 6.

Commence by borrowing two black hats. If there is an instrument in the room, ask some one to play a lively tune, as "eggs are fond of lively music to dance to." Then, with the brim of a hat in each hand, interpose the round of each hat successively under the thread that holds the egg, moving them from your breast toward the egg. The egg will appear to move of itself over the hats, as you place them under it.

You must not allow people to handle the egg on the thread afterwards, for when they see the simplicity of the process they will undervalue the trick, whereas it appears marvellous as long as they do not understand how the extraordinary movements are produced. And in these illusions, as Hudibras expresses it,

Doubtless, the pleasure is as great

In being cheated as to cheat.

FOURTH TRICK.—The Walking Cent.
PRELIMINARY PREPARATION IN PRIVATE.

Ask for a long dark hair from some lady's tresses. Have a pin in shape of a hook, or a small loop affixed to the end of this hair, and fasten a little piece of beeswax (less than a pea) at the other end of the hair. Fasten the hair by the loop to a button on your vest, taking care to wear a dark-colored vest. The hair may be allowed to hang from your vest, with the beeswax visible. Have a glass of water or cup on the table.

Commence the exhibition of the trick by borrowing a cent. While pretending to examine the cent to see if it is a good one, press the waxed end of the hair firmly to the under side of the cent, and place it about a foot from the edge of a table. Then bid the cent to move toward you, to the right or to the left, and by gently moving your body in whatever direction you name, the hair will draw the cent in the same direction. You may say, while your left hand is near the table, "Now, cent, move up my arm." Advancing your arm gently, the cent will appear to move up to your elbow. It is your arm that moves, but it will appear to the spectators as if the cent moved; or you may help it up the outside of the sleeve by interposing your right hand under the hair, so as to draw up the cent, while appearing to beckon it.

"Now, cent, as you have performed so well, you shall have a bath." Placing the tumbler near the edge of the table, draw the cent into it. After exhibiting it in the water, say, "Oh, cent, you must not stay so long in the water." Then jerk it out upon the table. Detach the waxed end of the hair by your nail, after which return the cent to the person who loaned it to you.

When performing this trick, in order to keep the spectators at a little distance, you must inform them that "the cent is very susceptible to magnetic influences, and request ladies not to approach too near it, as the loadstones of their eyes are the cause of the magnetic attraction."

FIG. 7.

My young friends must remember that it is absolutely necessary to keep up in spectators their belief in the mysterious, and therefore must decline on the spot to give explanations before or after the performance of this trick, however they may be disposed to reveal the secret privately to any friend. A singular instance is recorded of a person who was grievously disappointed when by importunity he had received an explanation of this very trick, which had appeared at first to him a most marvellous phenomenon; and he was quite annoyed when the gilt was stripped off his ginger-bread. It is said that a gentleman walked into a coffee-room at Manchester, England, and was exhibiting to a friend the above trick. A traveler at a table near them had his attention drawn by their laughing discourse, while one of them exhibited the trick to the other. The cold barrier of English reserve was broken down, and he addressed one of the strangers, requesting to be informed how the trick was done. For his part he imagined it must be connected with some perfectly new philosophical law of attraction involved in the experiment. "Will you be kind enough to tell me? I shall be happy to offer a fee to learn it. I was about to proceed by the next train, but I will gladly defer my journey to understand this, which appears so unaccountable."

The gentleman declined for a considerable time; but at length, being overcome by the importunity, in order to get rid of the matter, assented. The time of the departure of the train had arrived and passed by, and the aspirant offered two guineas to learn the trick. The gentleman acceded to his request on condition that he should faithfully promise not to reveal it to others, or to make public the mystery. "Agreed," says the traveler. The mail train was gone—the money paid—the trick exhibited and explained to him. "Oh!" cried the traveler, "how easy and plain it is. What a simpleton I have been to lose my journey and spend my money only to learn how you—." "Stop!" cried the gentleman, "remember you have promised not to divulge the secret." "Yes, but how foolish to care for an experiment which only depends on—." "Stop, sir, stop. Are you going to tell all the room?" and thus a good half-hour's amusement was caused by the traveler fretting over his simplicity, and having relinquished an important journey for that which, though marvellous while a secret, became so simple and uninteresting to him after an explanation.

CHAPTER III.
TRICKS WITH AND WITHOUT COLLUSION.

In resuming my hints to amateurs, I shall now offer some remarks upon two subjects.

FIRST.—I will notice the class of tricks that are performed by the collusion of a confederate. Old books on conjuring record several of this description, and some conjurors still practise them. But I do not advise the inexperienced frequently to exhibit tricks of this sort, for the co-operation of assistants used in them is liable to be traced by spectators, or to be divulged by the person who has been employed to aid in the exhibition of them. They may, indeed, be very well as a make-shift until dexterity of hand is acquired; but they will always rank as an inferior branch of the science of conjuring, and if the collusion is discovered, it will throw discredit even upon those tricks which the same performer may exhibit without such collusive arrangement. An instance of the annoying failure of such dependence upon confederates is recorded in "Houdin's Memoirs." It is there related that Torrini, at the commencement of his career, was insidiously induced by an envious rival (Pinetti) to undertake a public exhibition of his art before a very grand assembly. Torrini was at the time diffident of his own attainments, but he was persuaded to make the attempt by the assurance of Pinetti that he would take care that several confederates should be present, and should help in carrying out sundry illusions which he would have to display. One of these was, that the conjuror, after borrowing a ring, was to restore it magically into the possession of its owner. The ring was borrowed, and some mysterious gesticulations practised; but instead of the contemplated result being produced, the false confederate proclaimed aloud that he had lent a very valuable jewelled ring, and had only received back a common copper ring. The audience was of course disappointed at such words so derogatory to the conjuror. This unpleasant feeling was deepened by the malicious meddling of another false confederate. Torrini had to present some cards to the King of Naples, who was honoring the assembly by witnessing the exhibition, and a card was selected by his Majesty. Instead, however, of being pleased with what he saw on the card, the king manifested intense disapprobation. The confederate had written on the card words of disrespect and insult, and Torrini had to retire amid the loud censures of the enraged spectators. There may be no danger of so disastrous results to a young amateur; but dissatisfaction of a milder kind will probably ensue whenever it is discovered that any trick has depended upon the secret co-operation of an assistant among the spectators.

The SECOND topic which I propose at present to discuss is the employment of mechanism—such mechanical constructions as boxes with false sides, cabinets with secret drawers, or double compartments, etc.

It makes a great difference whether such arrangements are used as subordinate aids, or as constituting the essence and substance of the illusion. In the former respect it is quite legitimate to take advantage of any well-arranged mechanical aid subordinately. In fact, nearly all tricks must be performed with some modified aid of artistic contrivance, or with mechanical implements adroitly used. The conjuror, therefore, unavoidably requires, and may advantageously employ, mechanical arrangements to give greater effect to his illusions. I only wish to dissuade the learner from relying solely upon mere mechanical puzzles, or artistic contrivances, for furnishing an interesting exhibition of the conjuror's art.

The fewer the contrivances which he employs of this sort, and the more entirely the performance rests upon sleight-of-hand the more lively will be the surprise of the spectators.

I myself prefer doing without the aid of any confederate, and without mechanical aids; but I must remember that I am writing for amateurs and novices in the art, and that, in proportion as they are unpractised in palmistry, and in what the French term prestidigitation, (preste digite, signifying "ready fingers,") it will be desirable for them, at first, to have the assistance which mechanism will supply towards the exhibition of their tricks.

Let them, however, keep such aids as subordinate and as secret as possible. For instance, in the preparation for exhibiting the first trick described on page , the small tin tube (which is requisite for the performance of that trick) must not be seen by the audience, either BEFORE or AFTER the trick is exhibited, but must be kept secreted in the pocket. Again, in Trick No. 4, the preparation of the hair and beeswax must be made PRIVATELY beforehand; and these implements must vanish out of sight when the trick is over. And the reader must observe that in both the first and fourth tricks the mechanical aid employed is the minor and subordinate part of the tricks, and that a successful exhibition of either of them depends really on the dexterity of the passes, and of manipulations by the performer.

It may be admitted, then, that, with regard to the first topic of our present paper, the young conjuror need not be restrained from employing the subordinate aid of an assistant, so far as this may carry him over difficulties which he cannot otherwise surmount in the present stage of his imperfect skill.

And in regard to the second topic, the employment of mechanical contrivances, (though it may be well to begin with those departments of the art which are easier, because aided by mechanical apparatus,) it will be desirable for the amateur to strive to get free from dependence upon such aids. Mechanical arrangements cannot be wholly discarded at any time, and the conjuror will always require a few implements; but the more he advances in dexterity of hand, quickness of eye, control of his hand and eye, instantaneous adaptation of his words and movements to contingencies as they arise, the more able will he become to elude the observation of the most watchful spectators, and to mislead their imagination, so that they shall fancy that they see him DO things which he only APPEARS to do, and shall blindly fail to observe actions and movements carried out before their very eyes.

And here let me say, that I have, by long experience, come to the conviction, that the simpler and more common the objects are on which, and with which, a trick is performed, and the less anything beyond dexterity of hand is openly used, the greater will be the astonishment and the amusement of the spectators. There are, it is true, some very striking and complicated illusions which it is impossible to present without resorting to artistic contrivances of mechanical or scientific arrangement. On these illusions, as being beyond the power of a young amateur, I need not dwell. Nor need the preceding remarks be considered as any disparagement of the combinations and extrinsic aid which are indispensable for developing such startling illusions. The scope of my present remarks is simply to this effect, that to depend mainly upon the co-operation of a confederate, or upon mechanical contrivances, for what can be far better carried out by mere sleight-of-hand, will not pass for a satisfactory exhibition of conjuring now-a-days; and the amateur will find that, as he advances in skill and dexterity, he will swim more freely the less he trusts to such unsubstantial bladders to uphold him.

Having thus discussed my two topics I shall now add explanations of a few more tricks, which the learner may practise with the hope of making progress in the art of conjuring. The only way to make such progress and gain high attainments in the art, is to practise diligently over and over again the passes I have described in my former paper, and to learn to do a few tricks neatly, and without hesitation or stumbling. I subjoin, therefore, some simple but effective tricks, in which they will do well to perfect themselves.

TRICK 5.—To make a quarter and a penny change places, while held in the hands of two spectators.

PREPARATION.

Have a quarter of your own secreted in your right hand. Then borrow two handkerchiefs, and a quarter and a penny, from any one in the audience. Tell the lender to mark or accurately observe them, so that he will know them again. In placing them on the table, substitute your own quarter for the borrowed one, and conceal the borrowed one in your palm.

MEMORANDUM.

It is better to use things borrowed than coin of your own. Still, the conjuror should provide himself with articles requisite to display any trick, or otherwise much delay may occasionally arise while borrowing them.

Commence the trick by pointing out where the quarter and the penny are lying on the table. Take up the penny and show it openly to all. Then take up one of the handkerchiefs, and while pretending to wrap up the penny in it, substitute in its place the borrowed quarter which you had concealed in your palm, and ask one of your friends to feel that it is enfolded in the handkerchief, and bid him hold the handkerchief enclosing it above his head. Ask him if he has got the penny there safely. He will reply that he has.

Then take up your own quarter which was laid upon the table; pretend to wrap it up in the second handkerchief, but adroitly substitute the penny, (which you concealed in your palm while wrapping up the first handkerchief.) Ask some friend to hold it up above his head, indulging in some facetious remark. Slip your own quarter into your pocket. Clap your hands or wave your wand, saying, "Change." Tell your friends to unfold their handkerchiefs. They will be astonished to find that the quarter and penny have changed places.

TRICK 6.—Another trick with the dime, handkerchief, and an orange or lemon.

PREPARATION.

Have an orange or lemon ready, with a slit made in its side sufficiently large to admit the dime easily; and have in your pocket a good-sized silk handkerchief with a dime stitched into one of its corners.

Borrow a marked dime. Take out your handkerchief, and while pretending to wrap this dime in the handkerchief, conceal it in your palm, and take care that the one previously sewn into the corner of the handkerchief can be felt easily through the handkerchief. Giving it to one of your friends, tell him to feel that it has the dime in it, and to hold it up over his head firmly. While giving these directions to your friend, the dime that is in your palm must be transferred to your pocket, and introduced into the slit of the orange. Then bring the orange out of your pocket, and place it on a table; you will keep the slit on the side away from the audience.

Then make a few mesmeric passes over the hand of the person that holds the handkerchief, saying, "I will now destroy the sense of feeling in your hands. Tell me, can you feel the dime?" He will say, "Yes." You can reply, "Oh, you must be wrong, sir. See! I will shake out the handkerchief." Taking hold of one corner of it, shake it out, saying, "Observe, nothing will fall to the ground. You see that you were mistaken about feeling it in the handkerchief."

The fact is, the dime being stitched in the 'corner' could not fall out, and you must take care not to let that corner of the handkerchief hit against the ground. Put the handkerchief in your pocket, and say, "But I must return the borrowed dime." Exclaim: "Fly, dime, into the orange on the table." Cut up orange, and show the dime concealed in it, and then restore it to its owner, asking him to tell the audience if he finds it to be his own marked dime.

TRICK 7.—How to double your pocket money.

The only preparation is to have four cents concealed in your left palm.

Commence the trick by calling forward one of the spectators, and let him bring up his hat with him.

Then borrow five cents, or have them ready to produce from your own pocket should there be any delay.

Request your friend, while he places them one by one on a small plate or saucer, to count them audibly, so that the company may hear their number correctly. Inquire, "How many are there?" He will answer, "Five." Take up the saucer and pour them into your left hand, (where the other four are already concealed.) Then say, "Stay, I will place these in your hat, and you must raise it above your head, for all to see that nothing is added subsequently to them." You will have placed these nine cents in his hat unsuspected by him.

Borrow five cents more. Make Pass 1, as described on page 9, appearing to throw these five into your left hand, but really retaining them in your right hand, which is to fall by your side as if empty.

Afterwards get rid of four of the five cents into your pocket, retaining only one in your right palm.

Hold up your closed left hand, and say, while blowing on it: "Pass, cents, from my left hand into the hat. Now, sir, be kind enough to see if they have come into your possession. Please to count them aloud while placing them in the saucer." He will be surprised, as well as the spectators, to find that the cents in his hat have become nine.

You may then put on a rather offended look, and say: "Ah, sir! ah! I did not think you would do so! You have taken one out, I fear." Approaching your right hand to his sleeve, shake the sleeve, and let the one cent, which you have in your own hand, drop audibly into the saucer. It will raise a laugh against the holder of the hat. You can say: "Excuse me, I only made it appear that you had taken one. However, you see that the original money is now doubled."

TRICK 8.—The injured handkerchief restored.

PREPARATION.

Have a dime of your own wrapped in the centre of a piece of cambric about five or six inches in diameter, the ends falling down loose. Conceal these in the palm of your left hand.

Borrow a marked dime from any of the spectators, and a white cambric handkerchief. Throw the handkerchief spread out over your left palm, (holding under the handkerchief your own dime wrapped in the small piece of cambric.)

Openly place the borrowed dime on the centre of the spread-out handkerchief. Keeping hold of that dime, jerk the ends of the handkerchief over, so as to fall loose down from the lower side of your left hand. Draw out from between your thumb and fingers (that is from the upper side of your left hand) about two inches of the smaller piece of cambric, containing your own dime. The spectators will naturally conceive the two pieces of cambric you hold in that hand to be merely the cambric handkerchief.

Call any of the spectators forward, and request him to mark off with his knife the portion of the piece of cambric which holds your own dime, and whisper to him to cut it completely off, and to let the dime drop on the table. The spectators will believe that he has cut a hole in the handkerchief itself, and that the dime falling out is the one you recently borrowed, whereas it is in fact the other piece of cambric that has been cut, and the borrowed coin remains still wrapped up in the handkerchief.

Pretend to blame the person who cut the two inches off, saying: "Dear me, sir, what have you done? You have quite destroyed this nice handkerchief. Well, I hope, madam, you will pardon the mistake, if I manage by magic to restore to you your handkerchief in perfect order, and

I request you to allow me to try to do so." Carefully holding in the candle the edges of the cambric, (both of the part cut off and of the portion from which it was cut,) and letting the real handkerchief hang down from the same hand, pretend with a conjuring wand to weld together the edges of the cambric when they get hot, as a blacksmith welds metals together. You can prevent the flame from reaching the real handkerchief by tightly pressing your fingers. Then exclaim: "Oh, where is the dime?" and while picking it up from the table, get quietly rid of the pieces of cambric with their burnt edges into a hat or some corner unseen by the audience.

Holding up the dime which you had just lifted from the table say: "But to complete my trick I must replace this dime in the centre of the restored handkerchief, whence it was cut out."

Make the Pass 1, appearing to pass it into the centre of the handkerchief, but retaining it in your hand, and afterwards secretly pocket it. The handkerchief has already the borrowed dime in it. Say to the handkerchief: "Change—restore!" and unfolding it, show the borrowed coin in it. Shake out the handkerchief and show it is all sound and right, and restore it with thanks, as well as the borrowed dime, to the owners.

TRICK 9.—To make a large die pass through the crown of a hat without injuring it.

I will now give my young friends a nice, easy trick, requiring very little dexterity, as the articles for its exhibition can be purchased at any depot for the sale of conjuring apparatus; therefore the most diffident amateur will be able to display this trick.

PREPARATION.

Have a die exactly like the common dice, only it may be about two inches square. Have two covers for it, one of them exactly resembling the appearance of a die, only hollow, except that one side of it is open, so that it can easily be placed over, or be taken off, the solid die.

The other cover may be of decorated material, and it is intended to be placed over the first die-cover. Let this last cover be made of some pliant material, so that by compressing gently two of its sides with your fingers, while lifting it up, you can lift up the first die-cover, which will be within it.

Commence the trick by borrowing two hats; place one with its rims upwards on the table, and show that you place in that hat the die with its first cover on it. But say, "I forgot to appeal to the company whether they will like to see the trick done visibly or invisibly." They will most likely say, "Visibly;" but it is of no consequence which answer they make, for the process of the trick is the same in either case.

Take out from the lower hat the first cover, which is painted exactly like a die, and having placed the second hat (with its rims downwards) on the other hat, display the first cover, and openly place it on the crown of the upper hat. All the spectators will believe it to be the solid die itself. Then take your penknife; you may just thrust it into the crown of the hat, and pretend to cut all round the die-cover there lying; say—"I shall now bid it move into the lower hat, but it will not do so while uncovered, so I must place this ornamental cover over it." Do so; show that you have nothing in your hands or sleeves; then wave your wand or your hand, and say, "Change, pass, die, into the lower hat." Give it a little time. Then, compressing the outward cover gently, lift off also with it the painted die-cover, which it has inside it. Lift up the lower hat, and show the company the solid die lying in it. Show all that the upper hat has received no injury.

The illusion to the audience will be that the solid die has passed through the crown of the upper hat without at all injuring it. Return the hats to the owners, and show them to be uninjured.

TRICK 10.—To produce from a silk handkerchief bon-bons, candies, nuts, etc.

PREPARATION.

Have packages of various candies, wrapped up in bags of the thinnest tissue paper, and place them on your table rather sheltered from observation. Have also a plate or two on your table.

MEMORANDUM.

It will be always desirable to have the table removed two or three yards at least from the spectators, and of a height that they cannot see the surface of it while sitting down in front of it.

Commence the trick by borrowing a silk handkerchief, or any large handkerchief. After turning it about, throw it out on the table, so as to fall over one of these packages.

Having carefully observed where the bag lies, place your left hand so as to take up the bag while catching hold of the middle of the handkerchief.

Taking the handkerchief up by nearly the centre, the edges of it will fall around and conceal the bag; make some pretended wavings of your wand or right hand over the handkerchief, and say, "Now, handkerchief, you must supply my friends with some bon-bons." Squeeze with your right hand the lower part of the bag which is under the handkerchief; the bag will burst, and you can shake out into a plate its contents.

Asking some one to distribute them among your young friends, you can throw the handkerchief (as it were carelessly) over another bag, from which you can in the same way produce a liberal supply of some other sweetmeats, or macaroon biscuits, etc., etc., all of which will be duly appreciated by the juveniles, and they will applaud as long as you choose to continue this SWEET trick.

CHAPTER IV.
PRACTICE.

In conjuring, as in all other arts and sciences, perseverance is requisite in order to become expert and successful. There is no royal road, or possibility of acquiring the end, without exercising the means to that end. Let my young friends, then, carefully practise over and over again the passes and the tricks which I have already explained to them. It is the only way to attain dexterity and confidence, without which they will never be able to make any creditable exhibition of the art of conjuring. After they have attained considerable skill and sleight-of-hand in displaying a few tricks, they will easily extend the range of their performances, and gradually rise to greater ability. I may, therefore, parody an old injunction for obtaining success, and say: There are three rules for its attainment: The first is "Practice." The second is "Practice." The third is "Practice." In a word, constant and careful practice is requisite, if any wish to be successful as amateur conjurors. They should never attempt to exhibit before their friends any tricks that they have not so frequently practised that no bungling or hitch is likely to occur in their performance of it.

Let no one be staggered by the simplicity of the processes recommended in these tricks. The result will in fact be all the more astonishing, the simpler the operations employed.

The great point is the address of the performer, and that will carry through successfully the means employed. However simple and insignificant those means may appear to the learner when they have been explained to him, if there is good address and accurate manipulation, the astonishment at the result will be infinitely greater than any one would imagine possible to be produced by such simple means.

There is one help that I can suggest towards the better management of the hands in concealing or removing objects; it is the use of a conjuror's rod or short magic wand. This is, now-a-days, commonly a stick of about fifteen inches long, resembling a common rule, or a partially-ornamented one. You may often have observed this simple emblem of the conjuror's power, and deemed it a mere idle or useless affectation. The conjuror waves it mystically or majestically as he may be disposed. Of course you are right in your judgment that it can do no good magically; but it does not follow that it is useless. The fact is, that it is really of considerable service to him. If he wants to hold a coin or any object concealed in his hand, without others observing the fact of his hand being closed, the wand in that hand is a blind for its concealment. He may require to pick up or lay down some object, and he can do so while openly fetching or laying down his wand. If he wants to gain time, for any illusion or process of change, he can obtain it while engaging the attention of the spectators by some fantastic movements of his wand. By the use of the wand, therefore, you will be able to prevent the observation of your audience too pointedly following the movements which you wish to carry on secretly. You may also, at the same time, dispel their attention by humorous remarks, preventing it from being concentrated on watching your movements.

As a general rule, you must not apprise your audience of what you are actually doing, but must often interpose some other thought or object to occupy their mind. For instance: Do you desire that a person should not examine too closely any object which you place in his hand, tell him to hold it well above his head. That takes it out of the range of his eyes. It would never do to tell him not to look at it. He would then immediately suspect that you are afraid of something being observed.

Have you perchance forgotten to bring on your table any article requisite for displaying any trick, a feint must be made that you must have more candles, or must remove some other object, thus gaining the opportunity to fetch what you require without naming it.

Do not even announce too fully or vauntingly beforehand what is to be the result or development of any trick; rather proceed with it, and let the audience come unexpectedly upon a result which they had not contemplated. Their surprise will be greater, and their amusement more lively, at such unexpected result.

It is for this reason that it will be well to avoid the repetition of the same trick in the same evening, though requested to perform it over again. The minds of the spectators have already traced once the whole performance of it—the beginning, the middle, the end. The zest of it, therefore, is gone off; their minds are languid and disinterested about its second repetition; and the conjuror's art proportionately sinks in their estimation.

Having offered these general remarks, I will now invite the attention of my young friends to another batch of interesting tricks, which, with a little effort, they may succeed in exhibiting.

TRICK 11.—A sudden and unexpected supply of feathers from under a silk handkerchief or cloth.

PREPARATION.

Have ready a good supply of plumes of feathers. They may be obtained from a fur or fancy store, or purchased there loose, and tied up so as to lie thin and flexible where you wish to place them. You may have at least four batches of them. The common hackle feather will do, stitched round a thin piece of whalebone. Feathers that are a little injured for sale as ornaments may be picked up at little cost.

Take off your coat. You may then have one or more batches of feathers placed round each arm; the lower point of the stem on which the feathers are fixed being near your wrist, and the top of each batch of feathers confined near your elbow by a slight worsted string, so that they do not stick out the coat sleeve too much, or slip down together if two batches are concealed in the same sleeve. You can have one or more batches placed just within each side of your waistcoat, with the lower point of the stem within easy reach of your hand—about four inches below your chin. Then put your coat on.

FIG. 8.
Position 1. Position 2.

Commence the trick by borrowing a large silk handkerchief or cloth of the same size. Show it to be empty by holding out the two top corners in front of your breast, and shake the handkerchief while it falls loosely down over your vest. Then moving the handkerchief toward your left, catch hold (with your right thumb and finger) of the end of the stem of the plume, No. 1, and draw it from under the left side of your vest. It will remain concealed behind the handkerchief while you move your two hands to the right, which will draw out the plume from under your vest, then over the centre of your chest. Then toss the handkerchief about, enveloping the first batch of feathers; say, "Handkerchief, you must supply me with some feathers." In a minute or so, take off the handkerchief, and display the plume to the spectators.

Show the spectators again that the handkerchief is quite empty. Move your arms toward your right till your left hand comes just over the edge of the right side of your vest. With your left thumb and forefinger catch hold of the stem of the feathers there concealed, and by moving your arms back towards the left, you can draw out without its being observed the plume that had been concealed under the right side of your vest. Toss about and display as before this second batch of feathers, and then place them aside.

Then show to the company again that your handkerchief has nothing in it, and lay the handkerchief over both your hands. While waving it mysteriously about, exclaim that the handkerchief must furnish you with some more feathers. Draw out of the left sleeve one of the plumes, shake the feathers out while taking off the handkerchief from this, which will be plume the third.

Then, throwing your handkerchief over the hand, and clapping your hands together, (with the left over the right hand,) manage to catch hold of another point of a plume, and pull it out from your right sleeve while waving about your two hands with the handkerchief over them. You have now produced four plumes.

The exhibition may be continued to an increased number of plumes, if you have more concealed in your sleeves, or elsewhere; but four will probably be sufficient to manage at the commencement of your career as an amateur conjuror.

TRICK 12.—Heads or Tails?

I shall now give directions for reproducing, before a juvenile audience, a trick that will carry us back to the primitive style of conjuring in old times. I cannot say that there is anything very scientific or elevated in it, but, if neatly and adroitly executed, it will tell very well with a youthful audience.

PREPARATION.

You must take care that your table be so placed that none of the spectators can see behind yourself or the table. You must provide yourself with some young pet of the juveniles, such as a puppy, a kitten, or any other small pet. The performer must either have some little bag hanging under his coat-tails, or some provision for concealing the little animal behind him, or in a drawer before him; so that there will be no chance of any of the audience seeing it before the proper time. He must have ready also a penny, or any coin.

To begin the exhibition of the trick. Standing with all the nonchalance you can assume, and placing one or both your arms behind your back, you may say, "For a variety, I will challenge one of my young friends to come and try which of us will succeed best in a few tosses of this penny."

Induce some young person to come to the front of your table, and tell him to bring forward his hat. Ask him to toss first with the cent and put the hat over it, while you will guess "heads" or "tails." Say it shall be seen who is most successful in five guesses. After he has tossed up twice, you can take the penny, and say, "Now, I will vary the method of tossing. You shall name now which you choose, 'heads' or 'tails.'"

Toss up the penny, and while attention is occupied with this, and he is looking to see which is uppermost, heads or tails, you withdraw your left hand from behind you, holding the little animal you have concealed, and slipping it into the hat, and turning the hat down over it, exclaim, "Stay, I mean to pass the penny through the hat upon the table, and the whole affair shall be settled by the result of the present toss. You shall see the heads or tails on the table."

By Pass 1, pretend to place the penny on the hat, but retain it in your right hand. Say, "Fly, pass, and quickly." Lift the hat, and show both head and tail on the little animal or pet there concealed.

If you should have had a Guinea pig, you must make the guesses go on till your adversary guesses "tails," and then it will make a good laugh to say, "He has won, and he had better now take it up by the tail."

TRICK 13.—To cook pancakes or a flat plum cake in a hat, over some candles.

REQUISITE PREPARATION.

Have two gallipots or earthen jars, of a size to go easily into a hat, but of such dimensions that the one reversed will fit closely over the other. Tie worsted or a strip of linen round the smaller gallipot, so as to insure the larger one holding firmly round the smaller one. Have ready some thin, fluent dough, some sugar, and a few currants, enough for two or three pancakes or a small plum cake; also a spoon to stir the ingredients up.

Have at hand two or three warm pancakes that have just been prepared by the cook for you, with the same ingredients as mentioned above. Let them be firm and free from grease. Have also at hand two small plates, with knives and forks.

Commence the exhibition by borrowing two hats, to give you a choice with which to perform. You can remark that as you should be sorry to injure your friend's hat, you will secure it from being soiled by placing some paper in it as a lining. Hold up the paper to show it is only paper, and then openly place it in the hat, and lay the hat down on its side on the table near you, having the brim towards you.

Have the ready-prepared pancakes lying near you, and whilst taking off the attention of the spectators by pretending to arrange the articles on your table, slip the prepared pancakes or plum-cake into the hat.

FIG. 9.

Unobserved, also place the smaller gallipot in the hat, and while doing so, if requisite, add some remark, such as: "Please to shut, or open, that door," or any words that will draw off the attention of the spectators from what you are doing. You must next, with some parade, mix the fluent dough with the sugar and currants in the larger gallipot. It must be fluent enough to pour out slowly, apparently into the hat, but really into the smaller gallipot, which has been already concealed inside the hat. Show you have emptied the larger gallipot, all but a little; then, placing it over the smaller gallipot again, empty the very last of it, and press the larger gallipot firmly down over the smaller one. Then, with it, lift the smaller gallipot also, with its contents, while you appear only to take back the larger gallipot. Remove the gallipots, as supposed to be empty, out of sight. "Now, ladies and gentlemen, I must request your patience a few minutes for the process of cooking." Put two or three candles near one another, and move the hat at a safe distance above them for two or three minutes, making in the meantime any laughable remarks that may occur to you, such as: "My young friends will find this capital way of supplying themselves with a delicate dish when they have lost their puddings from being in the black books of their teacher or parents," or any similar humorous remark; but take care not to burn the hat whilst the (supposed) cooking is going on.

After a short interval, place the hat on the table, and with some little ceremony take out the real pancakes or plum-cake. Let it be cut up and handed round to the juveniles who may be present.

REMARKS.

A more finished or surer arrangement for holding the dough, etc., can be made with a tin apparatus, which can be prepared by any tinman, upon the same principle as the gallipots, taking care not to have it made larger than the inside of a youth's hat.

FIG. 10.

An amateur can render a common table more suitable for concealing any little object he wishes to have secreted, by placing three or four tumblers under each end of a plank, about the length to extend across the table, and throwing any common cloth over the board and table, or a kitchen table, covered with a cloth, having a drawer pulled out about six inches, will furnish a very good conjuror's table. It is well to have the table rather broad, so as to keep the spectators at a sufficient distance.

TRICK 14.—TO EAT A DISH OF PAPER SHAVINGS, AND DRAW THEM OUT OF YOUR MOUTH LIKE AN ATLANTIC CABLE.

PREPARATION.

Procure three or four yards of the thinnest tissue paper of various colors. Cut these up in strips of half an inch or three-quarters of an inch breadth, and join them. They will form a continuous strip of many feet in length. Roll this up carefully in a flat coil, as ribbons are rolled up. Let it make a coil about as large as the top of an egg-cup or an old-fashioned hunting-watch. Leave out of the innermost coil about an inch or more of that end of the paper, so that you can easily commence unwinding it from the centre of the coil.

Procure a large dish or basketful of paper-shavings, which can be obtained at little cost from any bookbinder's or stationer's. Shaken out it will appear to be a large quantity. As you wish it to appear that you have eaten a good portion of them, you can squeeze the remainder close together, and then there will appear to be few left, and that your appetite has reason to be satisfied.

Commence the trick by proclaiming you have a voracious appetite, so that you can make a meal off paper-shavings. Bend down over the plate, and take up handful after handful, pretend to munch them in your mouth, and make a face as if swallowing them, and as you take up another handful, put out those previously in your mouth, and put them aside. Having gone on with this as long as the spectators seem amused by it, at last, with your left hand, slip the prepared ball of tissue paper into your mouth, managing to place towards your teeth the end you wish to catch hold of with your right hand, for pulling the strip out from your mouth. You will take care also not to open your teeth too widely, lest the whole coil or ball should come out all at once.

Having got hold of the end, draw it slowly and gently forward. It will unroll to a length of twenty yards or more in a continuous strip, much to the amusement of the spectators.

When it has come to the end, you may remark: "I suppose we have come to a fault, as there is a 'solution of continuity here, just as the strongest cables break off,' so we must wait to pick up the end again, and go on next year, when the Great Eastern again goes out with its next Atlantic Cable."

TRICK 15.—How to cut off a nose—of course without actual injury.

PREPARATION.

Have ready a piece of calico of light color, or a white apron, a sponge saturated with a little liquid of the color of blood—port-wine, or the juice of beet-root, will do; also two knives, resembling each other, the one of them whole, the other with a large notch in its blade, so that when placed over the nose it will appear to have cut through the bridge of the nose. A cutler could supply such knives, or they may be purchased at the depots for conjuring apparatus.

Having placed out these articles on your table with seriousness and imposing formality, show to the audience the knife that is whole, and call upon them to observe that it is sufficiently strong and sharp. The other knife must be placed somewhere near you, but where it is sheltered from the observation of the spectators.

Ask some young friend to step forward, assuring him that you will not hurt him. Make him sit down on a chair facing the audience. After having measured the real knife across his nose, say: "But I may as well protect your clothes from being soiled, so I will put an apron round your neck." Go to the table to take up the apron, and, in doing so, place down the real knife where it cannot be seen, and, with your left hand take up the conjuror's knife, holding it by the blade, lest any one should observe the notch in it. Conceal at the same time also, in your left hand, the piece of sponge.

Advancing to the chair, tuck, with your right hand, the apron round the youth's neck. Then press the conjuror's knife firmly over the nose and leave it there, as if you had cut into the bridge of the nose. At the same time gently squeeze the sponge, and a little of the liquid will make an alarming appearance on the face and on the apron; go on for a short time, covering the face and apron with (apparent) blood. When the audience have seen it long enough, seize up the apron, wipe the face of the youth quite clean, throw away the conjuror's knife, and exhibit your young friend to the audience all right, and dismiss him with some facetious remark on his courage in undergoing the alarming operation.

CHAPTER V.
TRICKS BY MAGNETISM, CHEMISTRY, GALVANISM, OR ELECTRICITY.

There is a class of tricks about which I must say a few words, viz., those that require to be exhibited by the help of magnetism, chemistry, galvanism, or electricity. I need not dwell long on them, for I do not consider them such as the young people, for whom these notes are written, can be recommended to devote their attention to, for the following reasons: in the first place, they are, with a few exceptions, attended with considerable expense. Secondly, the tricks connected with the powerful agencies of galvanism and electricity are dangerous to the unskilful operator; and, even in experienced hands, the most effective of them are uncertain things to manage; therefore their effect cannot be depended on.

Some very interesting tricks have, doubtless, at times been exhibited by the help of galvanism and electricity. We have read of a conjuror by such help confounding a powerful Arab, by first letting him lift with ease a box, and afterwards rendering it impossible for him to raise it, when an electric current had, to his dismay, paralyzed all his strength. It is evident that an experiment of this kind could not be safely attempted by any but a very experienced person. We read also of conjurors who have surprised their audience by receiving them in a dimly-lit theatre, and then firing off a pistol, (to startle the audience and cover the real mode of operation,) they have by electricity lighted up one hundred lamps at once. This has proved very successful on some occasions; but on others, notwithstanding the most careful preparation and the greatest precaution, it has been found that the apparatus would not act, and the impatient spectators have visited the disappointing failure with their indignant murmurs. Other conjurors have become so attached to electric experiments, that they have proposed to regulate all the clocks of a large district by electricity, or have amused themselves by turning electric or galvanic currents to the door-handles of their houses, so that unsuspecting strangers, on touching them, were startled with electric shocks. There is also a trick for rendering one portion of a portrait electric by a metal plate concealed under it, and the spectators being invited to touch some part of the picture, have, on touching the spots that were charged with electricity, received a shock or powerful blow, as if the portrait resented their touching it.

Having briefly given the character of this class of tricks, and stated that they not only require expensive apparatus, but are attended with danger to the inexperienced, there still remains another serious objection, viz., that, like the experiments performed by automaton figures or complicated machinery, they are liable to fail, through any trifling disarrangement, just at the moment when the performer is hoping that his audience will be delighted with his surprising exhibition.

For these reasons I shall not stay to describe the more elaborate of these tricks, as, however interesting they may be to the scientific, they would not, in a youthful amateur's hands, be sure to produce the amusement which it is my primary object to supply.

The simpler experiments of magnetism and chemistry may well be regarded as recreations of science, interesting curiosities, suitable enough to be exhibited by a professor of chemistry for amusement and instruction; but even these can hardly be considered as belonging to "conjuring proper." Young people do not care, at festive parties, to watch red liquids turning into green, blue, and yellow; or the mixture of different chemical ingredients producing strange conversions into varied substances; nor will experiments that are interesting as chemical curiosities produce the same excitement and pleasing surprise that the wonders of sleight-of-hand do. In a word, such experiments in a private circle of young friends fail to constitute the most amusing kind of parlor magic, while upon a public stage they are too minute for any large audience to trace and comprehend.

Lest, however, my young readers should think that I have any desire to shut them out from any field of reasonable pleasure, I will now carefully select one or two examples of tricks connected with the sciences of magnetism and chemistry, and which may, even in the hands of amateurs, produce a safe and pleasing exhibition.

In the following trick they will find an amusing instance of the combination of science with rational recreation.

TRICK 16.—The watch obedient to the word of command.

The magnet is a well-known agent in producing several toys for the entertainment of the young, and though its attraction is wonderful, there is no danger likely to arise from employing it, in the same way as might arise from unskilful dabbling with electricity, galvanism, or chemical powers, and a strange and singular effect may be produced by placing a magnet of some little strength near a watch.

Supposing the young conjuror to have provided himself with a powerful but not very large magnet, let him conceal it in the palm, or under a thin glove in his left hand, or near the edge of the cuff of his sleeve. Let him then borrow a lady's watch, (without chain,) and the thinner the watch-case is, and if it has a glass, the better. Let him then call forward a youth, and placing the watch in his own right hand, and near to the ear of the other, ask him if he hears it going: he will answer "Yes."

Let him next bid the watch to stop; and on taking it in his left hand, where the magnet is concealed, it will stop, if held steadily; and on inquiring of his young friend whether he can hear it, he will reply "No."

Observe: you must keep systematically to using your right hand when you wish to make the watch go on, and to your left when you wish it to stop. Appealing to others among the company, the performer may then tell the watch to go on, and holding it in his right hand, and giving it a slight shake, apply it to one of their ears; it will be heard "tic, tic;" then holding it in his left hand and telling it to stop, they will also find that it does stop. You can pretend to doubt whether they are all deaf of one ear, but lastly may declare that this is caused by the obedient disposition of the watch, which so orderly obeys your command. Remind your audience that savages upon first seeing a watch believe it to be a living animal with power to think and act of itself. "At any rate," you may conclude, "the present watch seems to hear, to understand, and to obey my orders."

It will be an amusing addition to the above trick to say that you will now order the watch to fly away and conceal itself.

You must for this purpose have provided yourself with an electro-plated locket resembling a lady's watch, and have two loaves ready in some convenient corner.

When the watch has finished its "manual and platoon" exercise on the platform, you may say, "I will now place this watch visibly to all upon the table." Turn round to go to your table, and in walking to it, substitute the locket for the watch, and place the locket on some spot visible to all. It will not be distinguishable from the watch by the spectators at six or eight yards' distance from them. Conceal the watch itself in the palm of your hand. You can now exclaim, "I require two loaves," and walking towards them, slip the watch into the one you have prepared with a slit in its side. Advancing to the audience, ask in which loaf they will prefer that you shall bid the watch fly. If they name the one in which you have concealed it, proceed to break open the loaf and find the watch. But suppose they name the wrong one: you then, remembering that the left hand of the spectators is your right hand, proceed with the true loaf, whichever they have named, or manage to cross the position of the loaves as you place them on the table.

Then taking up the locket with your right hand, make Pass 1, as if transferring it to your left hand, but really retaining it in your right hand (as described in my first paper.) Blow upon your closed left hand, and say, "Watch, fly into that loaf." Clap your hands. It is gone.

Advancing to the loaf, get rid of the locket from your right hand; take up the loaf, break it open on the other side from that in which the locket was introduced, bring out the watch, and appeal to the lady to declare whether it is the same which she lent to you.

TRICK 17.

An experiment with a very mild dash of electricity in it, which will at any rate be a popular trick with most people that try it. It will do for a small entertainment, or at any joyous party of young people. It does not, however, require a large number to be present, but, contrary to the usual scientific tricks, its development comes off better with one companion than with a dozen.

PREPARATION.

You must induce your cousin Jemima, or some other young lady who is just of age to have cut her eye-teeth, to consent to help you by accompanying you to a room with closed shutters and no candles. A moderate-sized looking-glass must be on the table, the smaller the better, for reasons below assigned. Have ready at hand some ounces of hard candy.

You commence the trick by placing yourselves, hand-in-hand, before the looking glass. If it is rather small, your heads will be the closer—in order to see the reflection of both at once. Then, with mouths as open as may be, try which of you can crush his or her share of sugar-candy with the teeth the quickest. In the glass will appear the reflection of sparks of electricity, as the experiment proceeds. If your companion is nervous, you can of course support her with one arm—ladies are sometimes susceptible, whether from animal magnetism or what not. The electric sparks coming between the lips may also be attractive, and you may be tempted to try whether the electricity evaporates the sweetness; but of course you must not be tempted to forget the philosophical nature of the experiment; and, if you behave with propriety, the lady will doubtless, on her return to the company, tell them, in a staid manner, that the experiment was all right; and perhaps when you see her, even a day or two afterwards, you will observe there is an arch dimple on her cheek and an electric sparkle lighting up her eye—and I should not wonder if you should feel a desire to try the experiment over again.

TRICK 18.—A chemical trick to follow one where a young friend has assisted.

PREPARATION.

You must have a wine-glass, a saucer, and a teaspoon, and the chemical bottles No. 1 (silicate of potash) and No. 2 (aluminate of potash,) which can be obtained from any druggist.

At the close of some trick in which any young friend has assisted, you can say: "Well, my young friend, you have assisted me so courteously and well that I must, in order to express my thanks, ask you to take a glass of wine. Do you like wine? Ah, I see by your smile you do."

Pour out of bottle No. 1 half a glass, and, going towards him, stop short and say: "Ah, but I am afraid your mamma would be displeased with me if I gave you wine so strong without any water, and I should be sorry to tempt you to drink what she would disapprove. Stay, I will mix a little water with it."

Mix some of No. 2 bottle, so as to fill the wine-glass, and say: "Oh, never mind losing the pure wine; I dare say you will like it very well as it is," and make a few chatty remarks, to give the liquids time to mingle their effects in the glass; and after a minute or two say: "Ah! I'll tell you what I am sure your mamma would like still better—if I could give you some calves'-foot jelly. Now, I really believe, if I were to stir it with this teaspoon, and try my magic wand over it, I can turn it to jelly. Let us try." Occupy a little time while it is becoming like jelly, and go on with a little more talk till you see that it has become solid. Then say: "Well, after all, I will not deprive you of your wine; so here it is. Please drink it." Putting it to his lips, he will find it has become so solid that he cannot drink it, but it can be turned out quite solid into the saucer, and a general laugh will greet him on the disappointment of his wine.

Having submitted a few remarks upon the class of tricks that are to be performed by help of the sciences, magnetism, chemistry, etc., and having stated my reasons for my not more fully discussing them, I will now proceed to give an explanation of one or two more that are better suited for the practice of amateurs.

TRICK 19.—To draw three spools off two tapes without those spools having to come off the ends of the tapes, and while the four ends of the tapes are held by four persons.

PREPARATION.

You must have two narrow tapes of about four feet long, bent as in Fig. 11. Red tape I prefer.

You must next insert about half an inch of A through the loop of B, and bring it back down on the other part of A.

A spool such as cotton is wound on, or an ornamented ball with a hole drilled through it, just large enough to hold the tapes lightly, will be required (Fig. 13.)

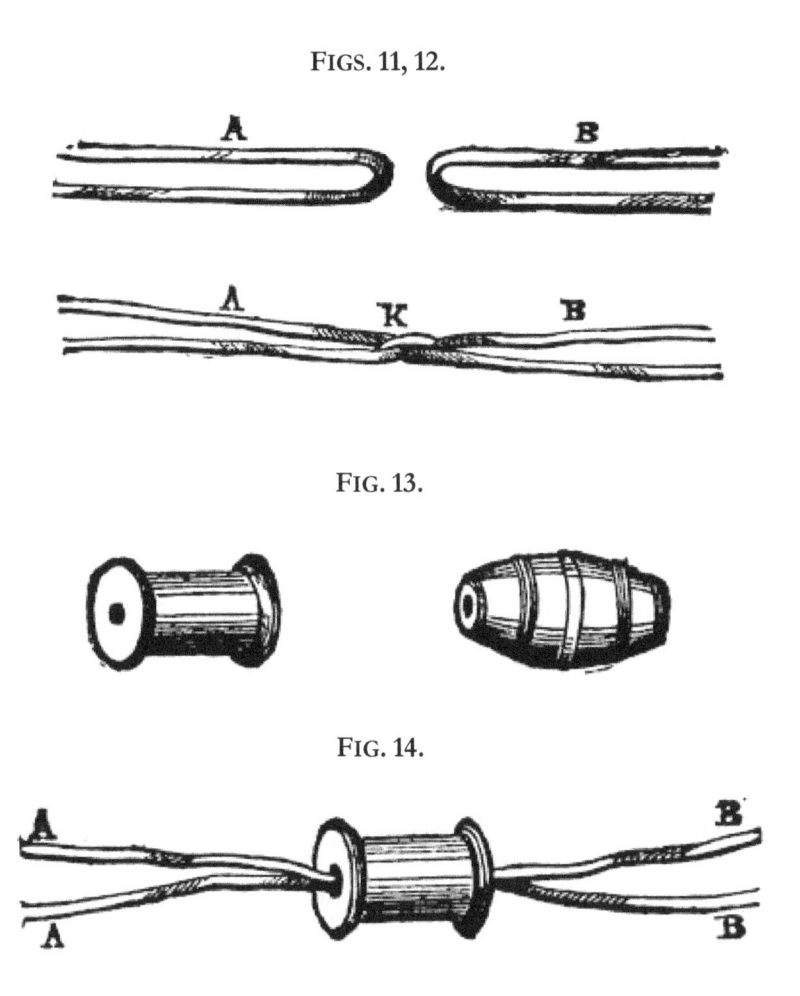

FIGS. 11, 12.

FIG. 13.

FIG. 14.

The spool or ball must be put on the tapes at the extreme ends of the tape B, and drawn to the left, till it just covers the noose at K. as in Fig. 14.

N. B.—All the above should be prepared before the spectators are invited to witness the trick.

Commence the exhibition by calling upon the spectators to observe that you hold a reel, or ball, through which two tapes are passed.

You may then produce two more spools, or wooden balls, and place one of them over the ends at A, and the other over the ends at B.

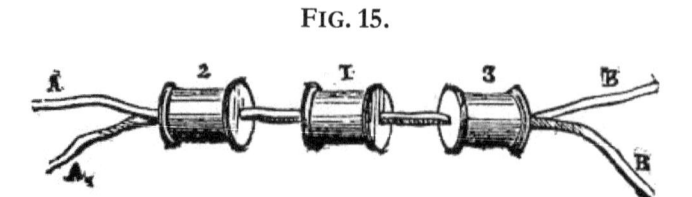

FIG. 15.

The following will then be the appearance of the balls or spools and the tapes passed through them (Fig. 15):

You may move about the spools 2 and 3, to show how the tape runs through them, but you must not move spool 1.

You may then say that the puzzle is to get the spools off the tapes while the four ends are held firmly in the hands of four persons. Appoint four persons to hold them, and you may then say: "To make doubly sure, I will tie one of the ends at A to one of the ends at B with (the first half of) a knot." It does not signify which ends you take to do this, so that you take one A and one B. "I will now pull these two ends so tight that it will draw the three spools together, and also tighten all along one side of them."

FIG. 16.

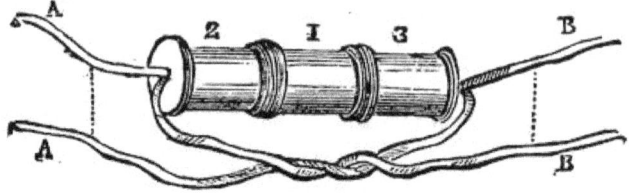

Then, while four persons hold firmly the extreme ends of the tapes, you must take shorter hold of the two A's with your left hand, (where it is marked by a dotted line, Fig. 16,) and also take hold of the other tapes where a dotted line is marked on them towards B. Then drawing your arms wider apart, so as to pull the tapes steadily, the spools or balls will fall to the ground without passing over the ends of the tapes.

TRICK 20.—To restore a tape whole after it has been cut in the middle.

PREPARATION.

Have five or six yards of tape about three-quarters of an inch broad.

Take half the length in each hand. You will be able to show the audience that you are about to cut it in the middle, by holding it in two loops of equal length. Call their attention pointedly to the equal division of the full length.

The tape will thus appear to the performer in the position represented in Fig. 17.

Observe the tape A crosses at z the tape B on the side next to the performer, whereas the tape D is to cross the tape y on the side farthest from him.

Fig. 18 represents the hands as they appear to the performer himself, holding the tape with the thumb and forefinger at the crossings of the tape at y and z, while the outward sides of each loop are to be held by the three other fingers of each hand.

FIG. 17.

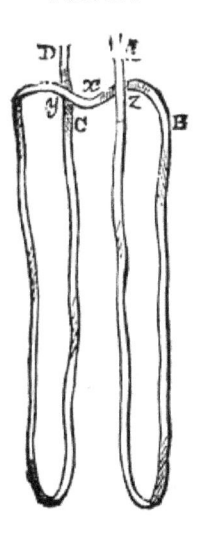

FIG. 18.
LEFT HAND, Right Hand.

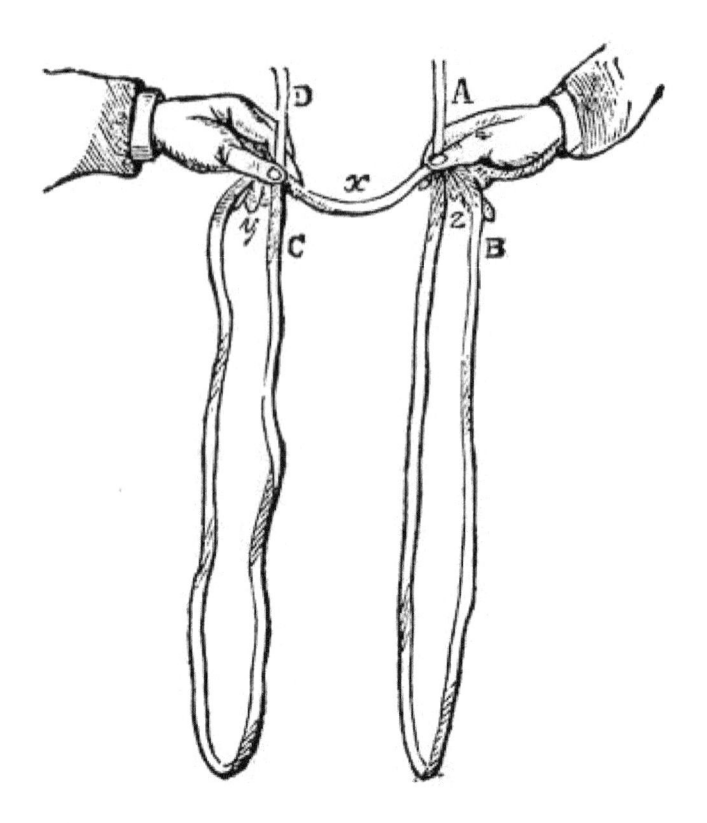

To proceed with the trick: Holding your hands in this position, (Fig. 18,) you must request one of the spectators to cut through the tape at x, but just as he is about to do so, you must quickly lower your hands two or three inches, and then raise them again. This movement will conceal the following operation. You drop the part (B) of the tape held in your right hand, and at the same moment pick up with that hand the other tape marked C.

This will bring the portion of tape from C to D, so that it now becomes the transverse tape, substituted in place of the tape marked x, and your young friend will then cut it—instead of the original tape marked x—without being aware that he is so doing.

When the tape has been cut through, you can put your hands near together, allowing the two ends of the little piece of the tape—C D—to be seen, but concealing from the spectators that you have hold of two pieces, one a very long one, and the other only about five inches long. You can then say: "Now I have to join these two ends, and to restore the tape whole as at first." You then turn the little piece C D round the piece y, which is in your left hand, and you tie a knot with the ends of that little piece. You must not tie this knot very tight, and after you have tied it, you drop the other end of the tape altogether out of your right hand.

FIG. 19.

The appearance which the tapes will then have is represented in Fig. 19. That is, you will seem to hold the equally divided pieces of the long tape joined in a knot at y, whereas in fact it is only the small end piece C D, tied round the middle of the long tape, which you hold between the thumb and forefinger of the left hand. Exhibit the knot to the company, and say: "I admit that this knot hardly looks like a perfect restoration; I must employ my best art to get rid of its unsightly appearance."

Ask some one to hold, at about three yards' distance, the end marked with small d, retaining hold of the centre—at y—in your left hand, which quite covers the knot. Tell your friend to wind the tape round his hand, and, while pretending to show him how to do this, by winding the part which you hold round your left hand, slide away towards your right the loose knot under your right hand. Then, holding out the end of the tape A towards another friend, to hold at about three yards' distance to the right, slip from off the long tape the little movable knot under your right hand, just before he takes hold of this end of the tape. Conceal in your right hand the little end-piece of tape, until you can get rid of it into your pocket, or into any unobserved spot. Blow upon your left hand, which is supposed still to cover the knot, saying: "Knot, begone!—Restore!" Take up your left hand, and show the tape to be free from any knot, or join from one end of it to the other.

CHAPTER VI.
ON THE CONTINUITY OF TRICKS.

It may be useful now to invite attention to the theory of preserving a continuity in the development of tricks, where circumstances admit of this being done. Sundry displays of legerdemain admit of being adroitly linked together; and I shall endeavor to explain why such an harmonious continuity is preferable to an unconnected series of isolated tricks; for when once a novice gets a clear perception of this principle, he will be able, according to his own special taste, to produce a pleasing variety of combinations in his experiments. He will thus rise above being a mere copyist of the methods used by others, and so will give a zest and freshness to his performances.

Now, there are many short and secondary dashes of legerdemain, which a spirited performer will be able to introduce in addition to the tricks which he is exhibiting. There are also several ornamental or fanciful little tricks which would not rivet the attention of an audience if exhibited by themselves. These, though unqualified to shine as the main object of observation, may nevertheless be worked into the evening's entertainment as amusing by-play, and may thus prevent the interest of the spectators from flagging. They may come in as accessories—as stimulating side-dishes—causing the entertainment to bear a continuous character, instead of merely consisting of sundry isolated experiments.

Let me be allowed to substantiate what I have advanced by reference to some of the tricks which I have already described.

The reader will have seen that, in some of the tricks explained in previous papers, there is simply some one definite object to be carried out. For instance, in the two tricks which concluded the last paper, the performer simply undertakes to throw the spools off the tape, or to restore a tape which has been cut. He sets about this, accomplishes it, and the trick is over. This is all very well as far as it goes. If the trick is really a good one, it is like a host furnishing his guests with a solid joint to satisfy their appetite; and it may do so. But still it comes short of a lively entertainment. It is confessedly dull for an audience to come to pauses or gaps between isolated tricks. Their attention is unoccupied while the performer, having finished off one trick, is making mute preparations to introduce some other trick wholly unconnected with what has gone before. Such a method will not keep awake the lively interest that the skilful combination of the conjuror's art will sustain. I maintain that varied by-play and supplementary sets-off will greatly heighten the interest of the performance.

It will also serve to disarm the suspicious and incredulous, preparing them to believe what they might otherwise stand on their guard against. Bare tricks brought forward as isolated experiments give time for the mind to take its estimate of their possibility; and, of course, in attempting to exhibit wonders, the improbability of them is apt to stare people strongly in the face. They are perfectly convinced that a dime cannot fly into an orange at the other end of the room, that ink cannot become water, nor a hat be safely used as a frying-pan; but if you interpose appearances and movements that are consistent with such processes going on, they are gradually prepared to recognize as a legitimate result what you have previously indicated as the contemplated end of those processes.

The amplification or fuller development which I speak of can be effected at any of the following stages:

1. In the introductory matter leading on to the main trick or transformation:

2. In the subsequent stages of its development; or,

3. In the winding-up smartly or variedly the conclusion of a trick.

I do not say that every trick is to be amplified or loaded with extraneous matter in all these different stages, (that would be to run into the contrary extreme of over-cumbrous amplification;) but I will endeavor to point out the effect of such development in the above three stages of a trick, and if I can show that amplification in each several one may be an improvement, I may be considered to have made good my proposition that any trick may be improved and rendered more interesting by one or other of those amplifications.

Let us see if we cannot lay down a bill of fare for our guests which, going beyond a solid joint, (good as that may be in its way,) will furnish them with some relishing accessory in the first course of a trick, some stimulant side-dishes with its second course, or may please with some bon-bons before the entertainment is quite concluded.

1. INTRODUCTORY.

Now, first as to introductory matter. Suppose a conjuror is able to perform Trick 3—the "Dancing Egg"—it will waken up his audience if, instead of proceeding at once with the trick, he can by sleight-of-hand find out an egg in the whiskers or necktie of some unwatchful spectator, and afterwards substitute for it the egg prepared with a hair and wax.

The chief aim of introductory matter should be to enlist the thoughts and expectations of your audience under your command, so as to preclude their watching what you are driving at. Show all you can safely show openly; enlarge upon the things being submitted to their own eyes and touch; engage their eyes and ears with certain appearances leading their thoughts to adopt your suggestions, so that, when you approach the development intended, they have had no reason to suspect your motives; thus having their confidence, you can jump at once to their credulity, though there may, in fact, exist some gap, or illogical process, which they omit to notice.

2. DURING THE SUCCESSIVE STAGES OF A TRICK.

I often vary and render more interesting the development of a trick by some little by-play.

For instance, in the trick which I often use as my first trick I make a candle an amusing helper, by snatching it from the candle-stick, and asking some one to hold it wrapt up in paper.

And this unexpected service of the candle is wrought into the body of the trick which I have in hand.

I change also a crystal ball into an orange by skilful manipulation.

By such brief diversion of the attention of the spectators, their eyes are withdrawn from watching too narrowly some manœuvre that is requisite to carry out the more important trick which you have in hand.

Or you may actually make an act, which is a mere accessory, cover some important portion of the trick; as in the tape trick (No. 20.) While PRETENDING TO SHOW YOUR ASSISTANT HOW TO HOLD the tape in HIS hand, you slip the knot away unperceived wider YOUR OWN hand.

3. IN CONCLUDING A TRICK.

It greatly adds to the efficiency of a trick to let it finish off with a sparkle, or some playful addition which gilds its exit.

For instance, in the trick of doubling the pocket-money, (7th trick,) the little by-play of finding, or rather pretending to find, some coins secreted in the sleeve of the young friend who has helped you, is sure to bring out a good-humored laugh at the termination of the trick. Again, in Trick 16, the additional fact of finding the watch in the loaf makes a lively termination of the performance of the obedient watch. In the 18th Trick, the glass of wine becoming solid might be used as a good finish to any trick where some friend has assisted in its exhibition.

You may often raise a good-humored laugh by appearing to swallow any object which you have used in a trick—as an orange, ball, egg, or dime—and afterwards bringing it out from your sleeve; or, by the use of Pass 1, to drive a coin up one sleeve, round the back of your neck, and down the other sleeve, into your right hand.

I not only consider such Amplifications of a trick lively and interesting, but I maintain this to be the best way of employing many secondary and short tricks wherever they can be brought in appropriately as offshoots of longer and more important ones.

TRICK 21.—The invisible hen: a very useful trick for supplying eggs for breakfast or dinner.

PREPARATION.

FIG. 20.

Position 1. Position 2.

In order to save the invisible hen trouble and delay, it will be advisable to have eight or ten egg-shells, (as described in Trick 3;) or some light imitation eggs, painted white, may be bought at any depot of conjuring apparatus. A linen or camlet bag may also be procured from the same depot, though I think a bag made at home, according to the following directions, to be preferable.

It must be about the size of a small pillow, two feet three inches across, and one foot nine inches deep. It has one of its sides of double cloth, (x,) the other single, (z,) in the same way as leather writing-cases have a pocket on one side, and a single cover on the other. The double side is stitched together all round, with the exception of an opening at A, which must be about five inches long, or large enough to admit easily a hand to put in or take out the eggs. This double side of the bag must always be kept towards the performer, whereas the single side must be always kept towards the spectators; and the only opening between these two sides is between C and D. On the interior of the side of the double cloth bag, a strip or kind of frill of the same cloth must be sewn, with an elastic binding round the pockets or cups for eggs. The elastic binding will keep them in these pockets, unless they are pressed by the thumb or finger, so as to release them and let them fall into the centre of the double bag. The strip has the appearance of a string of inverted egg-cups, thus:

FIG. 21.

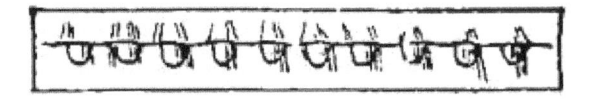

The position of it in the bag is indicated in Fig. 21 by the dots running across the bag; but the strip itself is never seen by the spectators, for it is placed on the inner side of the double bag, which is always towards the performer.

Having carefully prepared the above apparatus, commence the exhibition of the trick by holding up the bag by the corners C and D, as represented in Fig. 21. Shake the bag well while so holding it, showing it to be (apparently) empty.

After having thus exhibited the bag, thrust both your hands down inside it to the corners A and B. Holding those corners, pull the bag inside out, and again show it to be empty, in this reversed position, represented in Fig. 21.

As the spectators have now seen it thoroughly, inside and outside, you may put the question to them, "whether they admit it to be empty, as they ought to know."

While holding the bag by the same corners A and B, you must now gather the bag a little closer together, and holding it well up—see Fig. 21—press with your thumb one of the eggs out of its elastic cup. This can be easily done without any one observing the movement. This egg, with a little gentle shaking, will fall into the large bag made by the double side; but it cannot fall to the ground, however much you shake it, for there is no opening but at A, and that is upwards towards your right hand, so you may shake the bag boldly.

FIG. 22.

Position 3. Position 4.

You next lower the bag a little, and spread it on your chest, letting it rest there while you move your hands from A and B to take hold of the corners C and D; and you must give an opening for what had hitherto been the higher part of the bag, to drop through between the opening that there is between C and D. This will keep the double side of the bag (x) still towards yourself, and the bag will now be returned to its original position (Fig. 21.) With your left hand retaining hold of the corner D, and lowering the bag towards your right hand, shake well the loosened egg down towards the corner A. Search with your right hand about that corner, and the opening of the double bag, and you will be able to bring out the egg that had been loosened while the bag was in position 3.

Take out that egg; shake the bag well, as if it were quite empty: and then, thrusting both your hands into the interior corners at A and B, turn the bag inside out; bring it to position 2, ready to re-commence bringing out the other eggs one by one, as long as the spectators are interested. While you hold the bag in position 2, you can safely let any young person feel to the bottom of the bag, as he will not be likely to suspect the eggs are towards the top of the bag on the side near to yourself.

The same bag may be used also much to the amusement of children, by your loading it with walnuts, chestnuts, small apples, or pears, or any bon-bon of about the size of an egg; and then allowing the children, one by one, to feel in your lucky bag for what you take care they shall find in their successive searches.

A SERIES OF TRICKS, 22, 23, 24.—The chief agent being a plain gold ring.

PREPARATION.

You must be provided with a small thin wire pointed at both ends, which, being bent round, will resemble an ordinary plain gold ring.

You must also have on your table an orange or a lemon, a box or bowl, a tumbler, and a dessert-knife.

And you must have four or five needlefuls of thick cotton, which have been previously steeped for about an hour in a wine-glass of water, with a teaspoonful of salt in it; and have been afterwards completely dried, so as to burn easily.

TRICK 22.

Having the fictitious ring in the palm of your hand, commence by requesting any lady present to oblige you by lending you a plain gold ring, and borrow also from some gentleman a colored silk handkerchief. Appear to place the borrowed ring in that handkerchief, but in reality place in it the rounded fictitious ring. Doubling the centre of the handkerchief round it, request some gentleman to hold it, so as to be sure he has got the ring in the handkerchief—while you fetch a slight cord to fasten it. While going to your table to fetch this cord, you slip the real ring into a slit in the orange which you had prepared, and which closes readily over it. You then tie the cord round the handkerchief, about two inches from the ring, and, calling the spectators to notice how it is secured, take hold of that part of the handkerchief which incloses the fictitious ring in your own hand, and tell the gentleman to place one by one the four corners of the handkerchief over your hand. Directly he has begun to do this, your fingers must proceed to unbend and open the fictitious ring, and to press it by its pointed end through the silk, and conceal it in your own palm. You tell your assistant to blow upon the handkerchief and open it—the ring is gone, and you return the handkerchief to the owner. Fetch the orange from your table, and ask some one to cut it open, and he will find the lady's ring in the centre of the orange.

TRICK 23.

You are now to proceed immediately to the next development of the mysterious powers of the plain ring, which ladies so much admire. You may commence by remarking that "you have little doubt that this symbol of love and obedience will at your command pass through the table, solid as it is. Let us try."

Place the tumbler on the table—produce your own silk handkerchief, to the centre of which a plain ring is already fastened by a doubled silk thread of about 4 inches length.

Use Pass 1 with the real ring, as if passing it into the handkerchief: conceal that ring, and substitute for it the fictitious ring.

Then addressing the spectators, say:

"Now, ladies and gentlemen, I will drop this ring into the glass, so as you shall hear it fall." Do so. Let the handkerchief rest over the glass for a minute or two. "Now I must place this bowl under the table to receive the ring." In so placing the bowl, you must silently place the real ring in it. Then say aloud, "Change, ring; pass from the glass through the table into the bowl below." Lift up the handkerchief, and while inviting one or two to come and examine the glass and the bowl, smooth your forehead with the handkerchief as if heated, and pass it into your pocket. Your young friends will be astonished to find the ring not in the glass, where they heard it tinkle, but in the bowl underneath the table.

TRICK 24.

"Now, ring, you have amused us so well, that you shall, like Mahomet, be sustained in the air without visible support."

Place over a common walking-stick some of your prepared cotton threads, having twisted two or three of them together, and united them in a loop, which you draw through the ring, and then slip the ring through the end of the loop. The ring will then hang suspended about a foot below the stick. The stick itself may be steadily fixed, resting on the back of two chairs at an elevation, so as to be easily seen by the company.

When the ring has been thus suspended, set fire to the cotton about two inches above the ring; the flame will run upwards towards the stick; blow it out when about two inches from the stick, and the ring will remain pendulous in the air for some little time after the cotton has been burnt.

The suspension is said to be caused by a filament, or fine thread of glass—which has been formed by the ashes of the cotton uniting with the heated salt, with which the cotton had been prepared.

Now this trick would be too simple an experiment to be exhibited by itself; but coming as a finish to two other tricks, which have been performed with the same ring, the spectators

Will give it honor due.

I trust that I have satisfactorily established the assertion that a combination of congenial tricks will often tell more effectively than the same tricks would if exhibited without such combination.

CHAPTER VII.
FRIENDLY SUGGESTIONS.

As the amateur will aspire to come before his parlor audience some day or other, it may be some little service and help to him to give a few suggestions as to the best way of conducting such an exhibition, and to specify the kind of tricks to which he will do well to limit himself. It will be desirable to open with an off-hand expression of his wish to place before them a few amusing tricks to wile away an hour; and let him assume a lively air, for his own liveliness will sustain that of the spectators.

There are some conjurors who, though they can perform good tricks, exhibit them in such a heavy, uninteresting way that they create no enthusiasm. An over-anxious look, coupled with a creeping, fearful movement, and a dull, monotonous voice, will suggest distrust and dissatisfaction, even where the audience has come together prepossessed with the expectation of mirth and glee. Let none assume, then, to wave the conjuror's wand till he has himself some confidence in his powers, knows what he purposes to do, and means to carry it out. I would say that a moderate degree of assumption, a gay vivacity, ready to break out into a smile, a cheerful spirit, and a joyous voice, will go a great way to bespeak favor, which the performer can quickly repay by dashing off his tricks with enthusiasm. The language used by the conjurer should be studiously guarded. Let there be no vain-glorious assertions, no self-praise, but respectful deference to the judgment of the spectators; rather inclining to give them the credit of understanding more than they do, than twitting them with understanding less. Be neither overbearing with conceited "chaff" upon any of the company; nor, on the other hand, venture upon extreme and disconcerting compliments to any person present. Rather, as a courteous master of the ceremonies, conduct the experiments with a simple effort to please and to amuse all. With the exhibition of an amateur, the performance of some lively airs upon the piano by any friend will form an agreeable accompaniment, especially if the spirited and humorous melodies are introduced, which the public taste recognizes as the tunes of the day. You will do well to have your table neatly and carefully arranged. Let it not lie too near to the spectators, nor within reach of too minute inspection. It should be of sufficient height to show the main objects placed on it; but the surface of it may be just high enough to be sheltered from the spectators clearly viewing every article upon it. The ornaments should be few, yet, at the same time, be serviceable to shade a few articles which it may be policy to conceal.

1. The centre table may be a moderate-sized kitchen table, with a drawer to stand open; so that the performer can take any article out of the drawer with one hand, while engaging the eyes of the spectators with his other hand. A colored cloth should be over the tables, on the side towards the spectators.

2. Two small tables, at the sides of the centre table, may also be useful, as in Fig. 23.

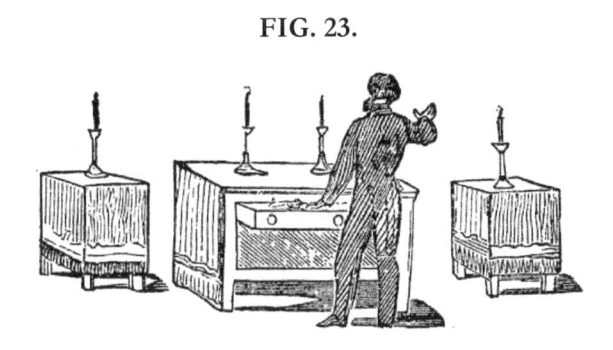

FIG. 23.

3. With tables arranged somewhat in this manner, the amateur will be able to take up articles, from either the surface or back of the tables, without attracting notice to his doing so. He must practise taking up things with one hand, while his other hand and his eyes are ostensibly occupied with some other object; for if the spectators see him looking behind his table, their eyes will immediately follow in the same direction.

The amateur will do well to select the simpler tricks for his first attempts, and never pretend to exhibit even those without having frequently and diligently practised them. He must make up his resolution to train his hands to the passes, and to the several manœuvres in the tricks, as diligently as young ladies train their fingers to the keys of the piano.

And let them not be discouraged if they feel awkward and nervous at first. Some of the best conjurors have candidly confessed their early failings and misgivings. With practice and perseverance this will, in most cases, wear off. I would augur that, if they feel an interest in the art, and a desire to excel in it, they will most probably secure a measure of success that will amply repay their efforts.

TRICK 25.—The Conjuror's "Bonus Genius," or Familiar Messenger.

This is an old trick that has delighted thousands, and may amuse thousands more, if adroitly performed. There are only the simplest mechanical arrangements connected with it; its successful exhibition depends upon the dexterity and vivacity of the performer.

PREPARATION.

You must have a strong wooden doll, about eight or ten inches high; the head must fix on or off by a peg at the bottom of the throat, being placed in a hole made at the top of the bust. Besides a close-fitting dress to its body, a large, loose, fantastic cloak must be placed round the whole figure, but must be so arranged as to allow the head to be pushed down through the part of the cloak that covers the bust, and an elastic pocket must be neatly made inside the cloak to receive and retain the head.

Having the above apparatus ready, you may commence by saying:

"Allow me, ladies and gentlemen, to introduce my learned friend and assistant—indefatigable in traveling to the most distant parts on any message I may wish to send him. He used to be recognized by early conjurors as their Bonus Genius—their good familiar spirit. But, whatever his special title, he is gifted with the art of rendering himself visible or invisible, as he feels disposed, while he travels to distant countries.

"Allow me to call your attention to the solid frame and unflinching nerves, at any rate to the well-seasoned constitution of my friend. [Rap him loudly, rap, rap, rap, on the table.] The raps he received during his education doubtless accustomed him to bear much without flinching. Though his travels have ranged from China to Peru, from the Equator to the Poles, you perceive he still sounds like a hardy Pole himself. (Rap, rap, rap.)

"I perceive, however, by the glaring of his eye, that, after my too rough handling, he is desirous of starting on his travels. I suppose we must provide him with the needful for his expenses. Large sums are given now-a-days to special correspondents in foreign countries; who will kindly give him sufficient? He will want a golden or silver key to open some curiosities he may wish to inspect in foreign cities. (Pause.) Oh, well, as there is a delay about it, I must myself supply him. I think I have a few disposable coins in my pocket: he shall have them."

Suiting the action to the word, while your left hand holds the upper part of the cloak near the neck, so as to cover what you are doing, you withdraw the wooden body with your right hand, while you move your right hand down to your pocket for the coins. You then leave the body of the doll in your pocket, and taking out the coins, present them to the head and cloak of the figure, which is held in your left hand, saying: "There, my good friend, you can now, if you wish, proceed on your tour to Algiers, or Dahomey, or Timbuctoo, or wherever the universal Yankee travelers fancy at the present to resort.

"Ah, I see he is pleased and in good spirits again. He wishes apparently to bid you good-bye. You will excuse his looking also round about him, to judge whether the weather is fair to set out; after which I will lay my hand on his head to express my good wishes for his journey. I dare say he will not stay much longer after that than a schoolboy does after his master has bid him good-bye."

Place with formal ceremony your hand on his head, press it down through the opening below it, receive it in your left hand underneath the cloak, and bestow it safely in the pocket.

Affect astonishment at finding the gown alone left in your hands, and fold it up with a lamentation at his departure. You may say: "It is clear that he has chosen to go to a hot climate, as he has left his cloak behind him."

Discourse for a few minutes about sending a telegram to overtake him at London or San Francisco—talk about the sea-passage, railways, tunnels, and what not.

"Ah, but I need none of these if I wish him back. I can summon him again by a few mystic wavings of my wand and by secret art. Hey, my friend, I need thy presence; quick, return, I pray you. I wish to see you again in your familiar garb—

By the pricking of my thumbs,

Something ghostly hither comes."

Swell out the cloak with your left hand, and at the same time thrust up the head from the pocket. It will appear as if the whole figure stood before them.

Then say: "I fear, dear friend, I have trespassed by abridging your tour. You can hardly have traversed Algeria, crossed the mountains of the moon, or found the birthplace of the Nile; and no one returns now-a-days without some such marvel to relate. I will let you depart again. As some people say to troublesome visitors: 'You may depart now; please to call again to-morrow.'"

Repeat the manœuvre, as before, of secreting the head. Then exclaim: "Alas! he is gone in earnest, like the sojourner of a day (with mock pathos.) When we have lost him, we feel our loneliness."

Fold up sorrowfully the cloak of the departed, and so conclude the trick.

TRICK 26.—The Shower of Money.

A dozen silver coins, or pennies, will be equally useful in exhibiting this trick; but some fictitious coin, in color resembling gold, will perhaps more effectively delight those who are charmed by the yellow glitter of the precious metal. The performer must have provided himself with so many of these in his left hand as he purposes to produce at the end of the trick, and two of the same coin also must be concealed in his right palm. He must further borrow a hat from one of the company.

The imagination of the spectators having been excited by the expectation of beholding a shower of money, the adept in sleight-of-hand, keeping one of the two coins in his right hand concealed, must advance the other coin to the end of his forefinger and thumb, while he pretends to pick a coin out of the candle, or of the rim of a hat, or from a lady's fan or shoulder, or may pretend to clutch a coin floating in the air. As he brings away his prize, he may rattle it against the other coin concealed in his right hand. Then, making Pass 1, he may pretend to pass it into the hat, being careful precisely at the same moment to drop, audibly, a coin from his left hand into the hat which he holds in that hand. Let him tell the audience to keep count how many he collects: it will rather distract their attention.

He can continue this pleasant appearance of acquiring wealth for ten minutes, or as long as he can devise various methods of appearing to clutch it, till the number with which he stored his left hand is exhausted.

He may then request some one to count out, audibly, into a plate the coins collected in the hat, which will coincide with the number he has appeared to collect so magically from various sources. When adroitly done, this trick is very pleasing and effective.

TRICK 27.—To Furnish Ladies With a Magic Supply of Tea or Coffee, at their selection, From One and the Same Jug.

PREPARATION.

Have a metal jug to hold not less than three pints. It must be constructed with two compartments in the lower part of it, holding about a pint and a quarter each, and these must each have a pipe connected with the spout of the jug and another pipe connecting with its handle, and in the handle a small hole about the size of a letter—o—in this print. These lower compartments must be filled with good tea and coffee before the jug is produced.

The upper chamber or compartment, like the upper portion of a patent coffee-pot, must have no communication with the lower divisions, and must be well closed also at the top with a tin cover, closely fitting. Have half a dozen small tea-cups and half a dozen small coffee-cups ready on a tray.

Begin the trick by placing openly in the upper compartment coffee-berries and tea, mixing them together. Take up, as a sudden thought, an old blacking bottle, and pretend to pour from it into the jug, to furnish highly-colored liquid to improve the coffee; and a little gunpowder, about a teaspoonful, may be fired off over the mixture to make the tea strong. Wave your wand over the jug.

Then you may address the ladies: inform them that the ingredients are well mixed, and invite them to name which they will prefer, "tea or coffee," as you can produce either at their command from the same jug.

Get some friend to hand the cups, while you follow him, and, by unstopping the holes in the handle for admitting air upon the coffee or tea, the one of them that each lady names will flow out from the spout of this magic jug.

TRICK 28.—A Pleasing Exhibition for both the Performer and the Audience to view when they feel a little Exhausted.

PREPARATION.

Have two pint bottles and one quart bottle; the pint bottles to be filled, one with a liquid resembling port, the other with one resembling sherry; the large bottle to be at first empty. Three opaque metal stands—the centre one to stand under the quart bottle, to have a large cavity to hold a quart, and the upper part of this stand to be full of large holes, like a cullender, for the liquor to run from the opening at H into that cavity.

FIG. 24.

You must also have three metal covers, of proper size to cover the above three bottles—these covers to have handles at top, so as to be easily lifted. The large centre cover is simply a cover; but the two side ones, which are to cover the pint bottles, must be made with metal cavities large enough to hold, one a pint of port, the other a pint of sherry, at top, with a descending pipe to fall into the mouths of the pint bottles.

FIG. 25.

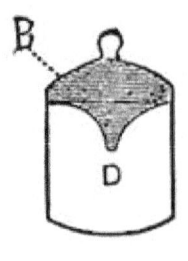

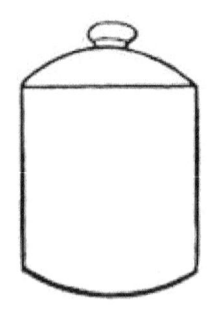

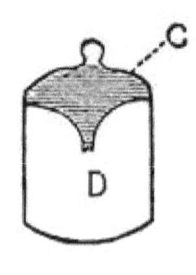

There must be a small hole at top of each of the small covers, at B and C, which hole, being covered with tinfoil, will, as long as it is closed, prevent the wine from running out at D. But when the tinfoil is scraped off, and the hole admits the air, the wine will then be able to run into the pint bottles.

The above apparatus being all ready, commence by saying: "I will now pour this pint of port and this pint of sherry into the large bottle, mixing them inseparably together." Having done so, remove the stopper at bottom of the large bottle as you place it on its stand, and immediately place the large cover over it. The mixed liquid will gradually run out into the concealed cavity in the stand.

You must now talk a little magic nonsense, to draw off the attention, while you place the special covers over each of the small bottles, so that the descending pipes in the covers fit in the necks of the bottles. Remove the tinfoil with which you had covered the holes at A and B.

With a few magic waves of your wand, and words of art, say: "I shall now cause the mixed liquids in the centre bottle to appear severally in their own original bottles." Let the covers remain a few seconds. Clap your hands, saying: "Change, begone!" Lift the centre cover: the large bottle will be seen to be empty. Lift successively the covers from the small bottles: they will be seen to have each their proper wine—one port, the other sherry.

TRICK 29.—To Furnish a Treat to the Gentlemen.

For this the magic bottle must be procured. One with three or four compartments is amply sufficient. In these place gin, sherry, and port wine, respectively. The bottle will have three or four holes, on which you place your fingers as if stopping the holes of a flute. You may have a bucket of water and a common bottle, resembling the magic one in size and appearance, near your table. Have ready also a tray of wine-glasses of thick glass, and holding only a very small quantity.

Exhibit the common bottle to the audience, and then place it on your table, and direct attention to some of the other articles on your table. "Now I must begin my experiment. I will wash and drain my bottle, that you may see the experiment from the beginning to the end." Place it in the bucket, and while shaking it about, and letting the water run out, exchange it for the magic bottle lying by the bucket. Wipe that carefully with a napkin, as if drying it, and calling two or three of the audience forward at a time, inquire which they prefer. Have the stops according to alphabetical order to prevent your mistaking—gin, port, sherry. Continue supplying the small glasses as called for, till your bottle gets nearly empty, and then pour them out indiscriminately. There will have been sufficient to satisfy the most eager.

But if you wish to continue the trick, yen may have a second magic bottle prepared in the same way, and you will easily, while propounding some magic charm and gesticulating, make some pretence that will enable you to exchange the empty for the second bottle, and so proceed.

VENTRILOQUISM MADE EASY.

WHAT IS VENTRILOQUISM?

Before we take the reader into the precise and minute instructions which he will have to study and practice ere he can become the possessor of the coveted art, it will be necessary to inform him what Ventriloquism[1] is, and in what it consists. In doing so, we shall endeavor to be as plain and clear as possible. Ventriloquism may be divided into two sections, or general heads, the first of which may be appropriately designated as Polyphonism, and consists of the simple imitation of the voices of human creatures, of animals, of musical instruments, and sounds and noises of every description in which no illusion is intended, but where, on the contrary, the imitation is avowedly executed by the mimic, amongst which we may classify sawing, planing, door-creaking, sounds of musical instruments, and other similar imitations.

[1] Literally signifying belly-speaking, from *venter*, the belly, and *loquor*, I speak.

Secondly, we have ventriloquism proper, which consists in the imitation of such voices,, sounds, and noises, not as originating in him, but in some other appropriate source at a given or varying distance, in any or even in several directions, either singly or together—a process exciting both wonder and amusement, and which may be accomplished by thousands who have hitherto viewed the ventriloquist as invested with a power wholly denied by nature to themselves. It is needless to observe, that when the imitations are effected without a movement of mouth, features, or body, the astonishment of the audience is considerably enhanced.

The terms polyphony, mimicry, or imitation, are employed to designate results obtained in reference to the first division of the subject, where no illusion is intended; while the term ventriloquism distinguishes those under the second division, where an illusion is palpably produced. The first is much more common than the latter; indeed, there is scarcely a public school which does not possess at least one boy capable of imitating the mewing of a cat, the barking of a dog, or the squeaking voice of an old woman. On the other hand, from a want of the knowledge of *how* to proceed, it is very seldom that even a blundering attempt at ventriloquism is heard, except from a public platform.

There have been many statements put forward defining ventriloquism, but we are decidedly of opinion that the theory of two of the most celebrated of foreign ventriloquists, Baron de Mengen and M. St. Gille, who were sufficiently unselfish to avow the secret of their art, is not only the most correct, but it is at once the most reasonable and the most natural.

From Baron de Mengen's account of himself, and the observations made by M. de la Chapelle, in his frequent examinations of St. Gille, whom we shall afterwards refer to, it seems that the factitious ventriloquist voice does not (as the etymology of the word imports) proceed from the belly, but is formed in the inner parts of the mouth and throat.

The art does not depend on a particular structure or organization of these parts, but may be acquired by almost any one ardently desirous of attaining it, and determined to persevere in repeated trials.

The judgments we form concerning the situation and distance of bodies, by means of the senses mutually assisting and correcting each other, seem to be entirely founded on experience; and we pass from the sign to the thing signified by it immediately, or at least without any intermediate steps perceptible to ourselves.

Hence it follows that if a man, though in the same room with another, can by any peculiar modifications of the organs of speech, produce a sound which, in faintness, tone, body, and every other sensible quality, perfectly resembles a sound delivered from the roof of an opposite house, the ear will naturally, without examination, refer it to that situation and distance; the sound which he hears being only a sign, which from infancy he has become accustomed, by experience, to associate with the idea of a person speaking from a house-top. A deception of this kind is practised with success on the organ and other musical instruments.

Rolandus, in his "Aglossostomographia," mentions, that if the mediastinum, which is naturally a single membrane, be divided into two parts, the speech will seem to come out of the breast, so that the bystanders will fancy the person possessed.

Mr. Gough, in the "Manchester Memoirs," vol. v. part ii. p. 622 London, 1802, investigates the method whereby men judge by the ear of the position of sonorous bodies relative to their own persons.

This author observes, in general that a sudden change in direction of sound, our knowledge of which, he conceives, does not depend on the impulse in the ear, but on other facts, will be perceived when the original communication is interrupted, provided there be a sensible echo. This circumstance will be acknowledged by any person who has had occasion to walk along a valley, intercepted with buildings, at the time that a peal of bells is ringing in it. The sound of the bells, instead of arriving constantly at the ears of the person so situated, is frequently reflected in a short time from two or three different places. These deceptions are, in many cases, so much diversified by the successive interpositions of fresh objects, that the steeple appears, in the hearer's judgment, to perform the part of an expert ventriloquist on a theatre—the extent of which is adapted to its own powers, and not to those of the human voice.

The similarity of effect which connects this phenomenon with ventriloquism, convinced the author, whenever he heard it, that what we know to be the cause in one instance, is also the cause in the other, viz., that the echo reaches the ear, while the original sound is intercepted by accident in the case of the bells *but by art*, in the case of the ventriloquist.

It is the business of the ventriloquist to amuse his admirers with tricks resembling the foregoing delusion; and it will be readily granted that he has a subtle sense, highly corrected by experience to manage, on which account the judgment must be cheated as well as the ear.

This can only be accomplished by making the pulses, constituting his words strike the heads of his hearers, not in the right lines that join their persons and his. He must therefore, know how to disguise the true direction of his voice; because the artifice will give him an opportunity to substitute almost any echo he chooses in the place of it. But the superior part of the human body has been already proved to form an extensive seat of sound, from every point of which the pulses are repelled as if they diverge from a common centre. This is the reason why people, who speak in the usual way, cannot conceal the direction of their voices, which in reality *fly off towards all points at the same instant*. The ventriloquist, therefore, by some means or other, acquires the difficult habit of *contracting* the field of sound within the *compass of his lips*, which enables him to confine the real path of his voice to narrow limits. For he who is master of his art has nothing to do but to place his mouth obliquely to the company, and to dart his words out of his mouth—if the expression may be used—whence they will then strike the ears of the audience as that from an unexpected quarter. Nature seems to fix no bounds to this kind of deception, only care must be taken not to let the path of the direct pulses pass too near the head of the person who is played upon, but the divergency of the pulses make him perceive the voice itself. Our readers will, therefore, not be surprised that the French Academy adopted this view of the subject, and laid down that the art consists in an *accurate imitation of any given sound as it reaches the ear*. In conformity with a theory so incontrovertible, physiologists have suggested a variety of movements of the vocal organs to explain still further the originating cause; and some have gone so far as to contend for a peculiarity of structure in these organs as an essential requirement; but they have wisely omitted to specify what. Nothing, however, can be more accurate than the description of "the *essence*" of ventriloquy in the "English

Cyclopædia"—namely, that it *"consists in creating illusions as to the distance and direction whence a sound has travelled."* How those sounds are produced, we shall show in another chapter,

VENTRILOQUISM AMONGST THE ANCIENTS.

Charles Lamb gave utterance to the thought that it was "pleasant to contemplate the head of the Ganges," but the student of ventriloquism finds it difficult to obtain a view of the source of his art. In the dim and misty ages of antiquity, he may trace under various guises the practice of it. Many of the old superstitions were fostered by its means; from the cradle of mankind to the birthplace of idolatry, we incidentally learn of the belief in a familiar spirit—a second voice, which afterwards took the form of divination.

The various kinds of divination amongst the nations of antiquity which were stated by the priesthood to be by a spirit, a familiar spirit, or a spirit of divination, are now supposed to have been effected by means of ventriloquism. Divination by a familiar spirit can be tracked through a long period of time. By reference to Leviticus xx. 27 it will be seen that the Mosaic law forbade the Hebrews to consult those having familiar spirits, and to put to death the possessor. The Mosaic law was given about fifteen hundred years before Christ. Divining by a familiar spirit was, however, so familiar to the Jews, that the prophet Isaiah draws a powerful illustration from the kind of voice heard in such divination, see Isaiah xxix. 4.

There can be little doubt but the Jews became acquainted with this voice during their compulsory captivity in Egypt. In many of the mysteries which accompanied the worship of Osiris, the unearthly voice speaking from hidden depths of unknown heights was common. Some philosophers have imagined that a series of tubes and acoustical appliances were used to accomplish these mysterious sounds. The statute of Memnon will instantly suggest itself as a familiar instance. The gigantic stone-head was heard to speak when the first rays of the worshipped sun glanced on its impassive features. The magic words were undoubtedly pronounced by the attendant priest, for we find a similar trick prevalent throughout the whole history of ventriloquism, and even now the public professors of the art know how much depends on fixing the attention of their audience on the object or place from whence the sound is supposed to proceed. The Jews carried the art with them into Palestine, for we trace the agency throughout their history.

The Greeks practised a mode of divination termed gastromancy, where the diviner replied without moving his lips, so that the consulter believed he heard the actual voice of a spirit speaking from its residence within the priest's belly.

In the Acts of the Apostles (xvi. 16), mention is made of a young woman with a familiar spirit meeting the Apostles in the city of Philippi, in Macedonia,—St. Chrysostom and other early Fathers of the Christian Church mention divination by a familiar spirit as practised in their day. The practice of similar divination is still common in the East; it lingers on the banks of the Nile, and is even practised among the Esquimaux. This divination by a familiar spirit has been practised upwards of three thousand years.

MODERN PROFESSORS OF THE ART.

The earliest notice of ventriloquial illusion, as carried out in modern times, has reference to Louis Brabant, *valet-de-chambre* of Francis I., who is said to have fallen in love with a beautiful and rich heiress, but was rejected by the parents as a low, unsuitable match. However, the father dying, he visits the widow; and on his first appearance in the house she hears herself accosted in a voice resembling that of her dead husband, and which seemed to proceed from above. "Give my daughter in marriage to Louis Brabant, who is a man of great fortune and excellent character. I now endure the inexpressible torments of purgatory, for having refused her to him; obey this admonition and I shall soon be delivered; you will provide a worthy husband for your daughter, and procure everlasting repose to the soul of your poor husband."

The dread summons, which had no appearance of proceeding from Louis, whose countenance exhibited no change, and whose lips were close and motionless, was instantly complied with; but the deceiver, in order to mend his finances for the accomplishment of the marriage contract, applies to one Cornu, an old and rich banker at Lyons, who had accumulated immense wealth by usury, and extortion, and was haunted by remorse of conscience. After some conversation on demons and spectres, the pains of purgatory, &c., during an interval of silence, a voice is heard, like that of the banker's deceased father, complaining of his dreadful situation in purgatory, and calling upon him to rescue him from thence, by putting into the hands of Louis Brabant, then with him, a large sum for the redemption of Christians in slavery with the Turks; threatening him at the same time with eternal damnation if he did not thus expiate his own sins. Upon a second interview, in which his ears were saluted with the complaints and groans of his father, and of all his deceased relations, imploring him, for the love of God, and in the name of every saint in the calendar, to have mercy on his own soul and others, Cornu obeyed the heavenly voice, and gave Louis 10,000 crowns, with which he returned to Paris, and married his mistress.

The works of M. L'Abbe La Chapelle, issued 1772, and before alluded to, contain descriptions of the ventriloquial achievements of Baron Mengen at Vienna; and those of M. St. Gille, near Paris, are equally interesting and astonishing. The former ingeniously constructed a doll with moveable lips, which he could readily control by a movement of the fingers under the dress; and with this automaton he was accustomed to hold humorous and satirical dialogues. He ascribed proficiency in his art to the frequent gratification of a propensity for counterfeiting the cries of the lower animals, and the voices of persons with whom he was brought in contact. So expert, indeed, had practice rendered him in this way, that the sounds uttered by him did not seem to issue from his own mouth. La Chapelle, having heard many surprising circumstances related concerning one M. St. Gille, a grocer at St. Germainen-Laye, near Paris, whose powers as a ventriloquist had given occasion to many singular and diverting scenes, formed the resolution of seeing him. Being seated with him on the opposite side of a fire, in a parlor on the ground floor, and very attentively observing him, the Abbe, after half an hour's conversation with M. St. Gille, heard himself called, on a sudden, by his name and title, in a voice that seemed to come from the roof of a house at a distance; and whilst he was pointing to the house from which the voice had appeared to him to proceed, he was yet more surprised at hearing the words, "it was not from that quarter," apparently in the same kind of voice as before, but which now seemed to issue from under the earth at one of the corners of the room. In short, this factitious voice played, as it were, everywhere about him, and seemed to proceed from any quarter or distance from which the operator chose to transmit it to him. To the Abbe, though conscious that the voice proceeded from the mouth of M. St. Gille, he appeared absolutely mute while he was exercising his talent; nor could any change in his countenance be discovered. But he observed that M. St. Gille presented only the profile of his face to him while he was speaking as a ventriloquist.

On another occasion, M. St. Gille sought for shelter from a storm in a neighboring convent; and finding the community in mourning, and inquiring the cause, he was told that one of their body, much esteemed by them, had lately died. Some of their religious attended him to the church, and showing him the tomb of their deceased brother, spoke very feelingly of the scanty honors that had been bestowed on his memory, when suddenly, a voice was heard, apparently proceeding from the roof of the choir, lamenting the situation of the defunct in purgatory, and reproaching the brotherhood with their want of zeal on his account. The whole community being afterwards convened in the church, the voice from the roof renewed its lamentations and reproaches, and the whole convent fell on their faces, and vowed a solemn reparation. Accordingly, they first chanted a *De profundis* in full choir; during the intervals of which the ghost occasionally expressed the comfort he received from their pious exercises and ejaculations in his behalf. The prior, when this religious service was concluded, entered into a serious conversation with M. St. Gille, and inveighed against the incredulity of our modern sceptics and pretended philosophers on the article of ghosts and apparitions; and St. Gille found it difficult to convince the fathers that the whole was a deception.

M. St. Gille, in 1771, submitted his attainments in this direction to several experiments before MM. Leroy and Fouchy, Commissioners of the Royal Academy of Sciences, and other persons of exalted rank, in order to demonstrate that his mimicry was so perfect as to reach the point of complete illusion. For this purpose a report was circulated that a spirit's voice had been heard at times in the environs of St. Germain, and that the commission was appointed to verify the fact. The company, with the exception of one lady, were apprised of the real nature of the case, the intention being to test the strength of the illusion upon her. The arrangement was that they should dine together in the country, in the open air; and while they were at table, the lady was addressed in a supernatural voice, now coming from the top of adjoining trees, then descending until it approached her, next receding and plunging into the ground, where it ceased. For upwards of two hours was this startling manifestation continued with such adroitness that she was convinced the voice belonged to a person from another world, and subsequent explanation failed to convince her to the contrary.

M. Alexandre, the famous ventriloquist, had an extraordinary facility in counterfeiting all the expressions of countenance and bodily conditions common to humanity. When in London, his mimetic powers, which he was fond of exercising both in public and private, made his company in high request among the upper circles. The Lord Mayor of the City, in particular, received the ventriloquist with great distinction, and invited him several times to dine at the Mansion House. But it unluckily happened that on every occasion when M. Alexandre dined there, he could not stay to spend the evening, having contracted engagements elsewhere. The Lord Mayor expressed much regret at this, and the ventriloquist himself was annoyed on the same account, being willing to do his best to entertain the guests whom the Lord Mayor had asked each time to meet him.

At last, on meeting M. Alexandre one day, the Lord Mayor engaged him to dine at the Mansion House on a remote day. "I fix it purposely," said his lordship, "at so distant a period, because I wish to make sure this time of your remaining with us through the evening." Through fear of seeming purposely to slight his lordship, M. Alexandre did not dare to tell the Mayor that on that very morning he had accepted an invitation from a nobleman of high rank to spend at his house the evening of the identical day so unfortunately pitched on by the civic dignitary. All the ventriloquist said in reply was, "I promise, my lord to remain at the Mansion House, till you, yourself think it time for me to take my leave." "Ah, well," said the Lord Mayor, and he went off perfectly satisfied.

At the appointed day Alexandre sat himself down at the magistrate's board. Never had the ventriloquist comported himself with so much spirit and gaiety. He insisted on devoting bumpers to each and every lady present.

The toasts went round, the old port flowed like water, and the artiste in particular seemed in danger of loosing his reason under its potent influence. When others stopped, he stopped not, but continued filling and emptying incessantly. By and by, his eyes began to stare, his visage became purple, his tongue grew confused, his whole body seemed to steam of wine, and finally he sank from his chair in a state of maudlin, helpless insensibility.

Regretting the condition of his guest, the Lord Mayor got him quietly lifted, and conveyed to his own carriage, giving orders for him to be taken home to his lodgings. As soon as M. Alexandre was deposited there, he became a very different being. It was now ten o'clock, and but half an hour was left to him to prepare for his appointed visit to the Duke of ——'s *soiree*. The ventriloquist disrobed himself, taking first from his breast a quantity of sponge which he had placed beneath his waist coat, and into the pores of which he had, with a quick and dexterous hand, poured the greater portion of the wine which he had apparently swallowed.

Having washed from his person all tokens of his simulated intoxication, and dressed himself anew, M. Alexandre then betook himself to the mansion of the nobleman to whom he had engaged himself.

On the following day the fashionable newspapers gave a detailed account of the grand party at his Grace the Duke of ——'s, and eulogized to the skies the entertaining performances of M. Alexandre, who, they said, had surpassed himself on this occasion. Some days afterwards, the Lord Mayor encountered M. Alexandre. "Ah, how are you?" said his lordship. "Very well, my lord," was the reply. "Our newspapers are pretty pieces of veracity," said his lordship. "Have you seen the *Courier* of the other day? Why, it makes you out to have exhibited in great style last Thursday night at his Grace of ——'s!" "It has but told the truth," said the mimic. "What? impossible!" cried the Mayor. "You do not remember, then, the state into which you unfortunately got at the Mansion House?" And thereupon the worthy magistrate detailed to the ventriloquist the circumstances of his intoxication, and the care that had been taken with him, with other points of the case. M. Alexandre heard his lordship to an end, and then confessed the stratagem which he had played off, and the cause of it.

"I had promised," said Alexandre, "to be with his Grace at half-past ten. I had also promised not to leave you till you yourself considered it fit time.

I kept my word in both cases—you know the way." The civic functionary laughed heartily, and on the following evening Alexandre made up for his trick by making the Mansion House ring with laughter till daylight.

Many anecdotes are told respecting M. Alexandre's power of assuming the faces of other people. At Abbotsford, during a visit there, he actually sat to a sculptor five times in the character of a noted clergyman, with whose real features the sculptor was well acquainted. When the sittings were closed and the bust modelled, the mimic cast off his wig and assumed dress, and appeared with his own natural countenance, to the terror almost of the sculptor, and to the great amusement of Sir Walter and others who had been in the secret.

Of this most celebrated ventriloquist it is related that on one occasion he was passing along the Strand, when a friend desired a specimen of his abilities. At this instant a load of hay was passing along near Temple Bar, when Alexandre called attention to the suffocating cries of a man in the centre of the hay. A crowd gathered round and stopped the astonished carter, and demanded why he was carrying a fellow-creature in his hay. The complaints and cries of the smothered man now became painful, and there was every reason to believe that he was dying. The crowd, regardless of the stoppage to the traffic, instantly proceeded to unload the hay into the street. The smothered voice urged them to make haste, but the feelings of the people may be imagined when the cart was empty and nobody was found, while Alexandre and his friend walked off laughing at the unexpected results of their trick.

It would be obviously invidious to compare the merits of living professors. Mr. Maccabe, Mr. Gallagher, Mr. Thurton and Mr. Macmillan have long been favorites with the public.

THE THEORY OF VENTRILOQUISM.

Many physiologists aver that ventriloquism is obtained by speaking during the inspiration of air. It is quite possible to articulate under these circumstances, and the plan may with advantage be occasionally adopted; but our own practical experience and close observation of many public performers, and of not a few private friends who have attained distinctness and no small amount of facility in the art, convince us that the general current of utterance is, as in ordinary speech, during *expiration* of the breath. Some imagine that the means of procuring the required imitation are comprised in a thorough management of the echoes of sound. Unfortunately, however, for this theory, an echo only repeats what has been already brought into existence. Several eminent ventriloquists, including the late Mr. Matthews, have displayed the vocal illusion while walking in the streets. Baron Mengen describes as follows his mode of speaking, when he desired the illusion to take the direction of a voice emanating from the doll: "*I press my tongue against the teeth, and then circumscribe a cavity between my left cheek and teeth, in which the voice is produced by the air held in reserve in the pharynx.* The sounds thus receive a hollow and muffled tone, which causes them to appear to come from a distance." The Baron furthermore mentions that it is essential to have the breath well under control, and not to respire more than can be avoided. M. St. Gille was seen to look somewhat exhausted when the vocal illusion grew less perfect. We ourselves, and all ventriloquists with whom we have conferred, have acknowledged that they have experienced fatigue in the chest, and have attributed it to the slow expiration of the breath. M. St. Gille, with the majority of ventriloquists, was often compelled to cough during the progress of his exercitation.

To attain an exact and positive knowledge of the modifications of voice specified as ventriloquism, it is important to be familiar with the distinctions of the sounds uttered by the mouth; and to ascertain how the organs act in producing those vocal modifications, it is necessary to know how the breath is vocalized in all distinctions of pitch, loudness, and quality, by the ordinary actions of the vocal organs. In ordinary language, we speak of noise, of common sound, and of musical sound-terms employed by Dr. Thomas Young in illustrating the mechanical agencies of articulation:—"A quill striking against a piece of wood causes a noise, but striking successively against the teeth of a wheel, or of a comb, a continued sound, and, if the teeth of the wheel are at equal distances, and the velocity of the rotation is constant, a musical sound. The general terms—pitch, loudness, quality, and duration, embrace all the distinctions with which the musician has to deal, and which he uses in his art."

The distinguishing feature of musical sound is its uniform pitch throughout its duration, and acoustically musical sound is composed of an equal number of impulses or noises produced in equal tones.

The general terms—pitch, loudness, quality, and duration, also embrace all the distinctions heard in ordinary sounds. These sounds differ from the musical in the pitch constantly varying throughout their duration, as the human voice in speaking, and the voice of quadrupeds. Acoustically such sounds are composed of an unequal number of impulses or noises produced in equal tones. And from this circumstance pitch, in the strictly musical sense, is not a property of ordinary sound.

The general terms—loudness and quality, embrace all the distinctions heard in a noise, as in the collision of two unelastic sticks. Pitch and duration can scarcely be considered as belonging to common noise. Thus we have—(1) noise whose audible distinctions are comprehended under the general terms loudness and quality; (2) common sound, whose audible distinctions are comprehended under the general terms—loudness, quality, duration, and every varying pitch; (3) musical sound, whose audible distinctions are comprehended under the general terms—loudness, quality, duration, and uniform pitch.

Phonation, or the production of voice, is a result of actions taking place under two distinct classes of laws—namely, the ordinary mechanical laws of acoustics, and the physiological laws of muscular movement. The adjustment of the vocal mechanism to be brought into operation by the current of air, is made by actions under the latter laws; and phonation is the result of the reaction of the mechanism on the current of air, by mechanical movements under the former laws. Now, the pitch of the voice essentially depends on the tension of the vocal ligaments; the loudness or the extent of the excursion of these ligaments in their vibration; the duration on the continuance of the vocalizing causes; the quality on the organization of the larynx, and also on the form and size of the vocal tube. The form and size of this tube can be altered in various ways—for instance, by dilating or contracting the pharynx; by dilating or contracting the mouth; by contracting the communication between the pharynx and mouth, so as to constitute them distinct chambers, or by dilating the opening so as to throw them into one, which is chiefly attained by movements of the soft palate; and by altering the form of the mouth's cavity, which is effected by varying the position of the tongue. Each of these modifications of the vocal tube conveys a peculiarity of quality to the voice,—all, however, being local or laryngeal sounds. Moreover, sounds can be produced in the vocal tube, apart from the larynx. These, strictly speaking, are not vocal sounds, though some of them may be of a definite and uniform pitch, while others are mere noises—as rustling, whispering, gurgling, whistling, snoring, and the like. Now, as everything audible comes under the classes of noise, sound, or musical sound, and as each variety originates in the vocal apparatus of man, it is obvious that *an ordinary vocal apparatus is all that is required for the achievement of the feats* of ventriloquism.

A person having an ear acutely perceptive to the nice distinctions of sounds, may, by a little practice, imitate many sounds with accuracy. Those persons, however, who are highly endowed with the mental requisites, which consist of an intense desire to mimic, coupled with the ability to originate mimetic ideas, are able to imitate sounds at first hearing.

We next proceed to treat of those illusions, where the voice so perfectly counterfeits the reality intended, that it appears not to issue from the mimic, but from an appropriate source, in whatever direction, and at whatever distance the source may be. We do not hear the distance which a sound has travelled from its source, but we judge the distance from our former experience, by comparing the loudness which we hear with the known distance and known loudness of similar sounds heard on former occasions. Common experience will prove that we oftener err in estimating the distance of uncommon than of familiar sounds. In apology for such an error, the ordinary language is, "It seemed too loud to come so far," or "It seemed too near to be so faint a sound," as the case may be,—both of which are apologies for an erroneous judgment, and not for faulty hearing. Near sounds are louder than distant ones. Now, by preserving the same *pitch*, *quality*, and *duration*, but with an *accurately graduated reduction of loudness*, a series forming a *perspective* of sounds may be created, which, falling in succession on the ear, will suggest to the mind a constantly increasing distance of the sound's source. The estimate, then, which is formed of the distance which a sound has travelled before reaching the ear is a judgment of the mind formed by comparing a present perception (by hearing) with the remembrance of a former loudness in connection with its known distance. With regard to direction, it is observed, "The direction whence a sound comes seems to be judged of by the right of left ear receiving the stronger impression, which, however, can only take place when the sound's source is in a plane, or nearly so, with a line passing through both ears. It is familiarly known that a person in a house cannot by the noise of an approaching carriage judge with certainty whether it is coming from the right or left. He accurately judges it to be approaching, passing, or receding, as the case may be, by the gradations of loudness, but is unable to decide with certainty whether its approach or recession is from up or down the street. Enough has been stated to show that we do not *hear*, but that we judge *the direction a sound has travelled from its source on reaching the ear.*" The ventriloquist indicates, either directly or indirectly, the direction from which he wishes his audience to believe the sound is coming. Thus he directly indicates it by words, such as—"Are you up there?" "He is up the chimney," "He is in the cellar," "Are you down there?" &c., as illustrated in the various examples. He indirectly indicates it by some suggestive circumstance, as an action or gesture, which is so skilfully unobtrusive and natural as to effect its object without being discovered. Thus, when the ventriloquist looks or listens in any direction, or even simply turns towards any point, as if he expected sound to come thence, *the attention of an audience is by that means instantly directed also to the same place.* Thus, before a sound is produced, the audience expect it to come in the *suggested direction*; and the ventriloquist has merely, by his *adjustment of vocal loudness*, to indicate the necessary distance, when a *misjudgment of the audience will complete the illusion which he has begun.*

The effect which is produced on sound by its travelling from a distance, is observed to be:—

(1) That its loudness is reduced in proportion to its distance.

(2) That its *pitch* remains unaltered.

(3) That its *quality* or *tone* is somewhat altered.

(4) That its duration remains unaltered.

(5) That the human speech is *somewhat obscured*, chiefly in the *consonant* sounds.

It must be remembered that the ventriloquist makes the sound, not as it is heard at its source, *but as it is heard after travelling from a distance.*

THE MEANS BY WHICH IT IS EFFECTED.

Before entering upon the first and easy lessons, it will be as well to consider the means by which the effect is produced. The Student is supposed to have made himself thoroughly acquainted with the previous chapter, as to the effect to be produced, *not on himself,* but *on the spectators and audience.* And we may assure him, that if he has a fair range of voice, a diligent observance of the rules which we are about to lay down, coupled with attention to the nature of sound as it falls upon the ear, will lead him to such triumphs as, in all probability, he never imagined he could have attained—an assurance which we are emboldened to offer from *our own pursuit and practical realization of the art.*

The student must bear in mind that the means are *simply natural ones*, used in accordance with *natural laws*. We have given him the acoustical theory of the effect on the auric nerve, and the means are the organs of respiration and sound, with the adjoining muscles. They are the diaphragm, the lungs, the trachea, the larynx, the pharynx, and the mouth. The diaphragm is a very large convex muscle, situated below the lungs, and having full power over respiration. The lungs are the organs of respiration, and are seated at each side of the chest; they consist of air-tubes minutely ramified in a loose tissue, and terminating in very small sacs, termed air-cells. The trachea is a tube, the continuation of the larynx, commonly called the windpipe: through this the air passes to and from the lungs. It is formed of cartilaginous rings, by means of which it may be elongated or shortened. The larynx is that portion of the air-tube immediately above the trachea: its position is indicated by a large projection in the throat. In the interior of this part of the throat are situated the vocal chords. They are four bands of elastic substance somewhat similar to India-rubber. The cavity, or opening between these vocal chords is called the glottis: it possesses the power of expanding or contracting under the influence of the muscles of the larynx. The pharynx is a cavity above the larynx, communicating with the nasal passages: it is partially visible when the mouth is opened and the tongue lowered. Near this part of the root of the tongue is situated the epiglottis, which acts as a lid or cover in closing over the air-tube during the act of swallowing. The mouth forms a cavity to reflect and strengthen the resonance of the vibrations produced in the air-tube; it also possesses numberless minute powers of contraction and modification.

We now proceed to give the instructions to which we have referred—instructions guaranteed by a proficiency which we are ever ready to submit to the ordeal of a critical examination, either in private or in public.

If the student will pay strict attention to the parts printed in *italics*, and will practice the voices here specified, he will find that they are the *key to all imitative sounds and voices*; and, according to the range of his voice and the capabilities of his mimetic power, he will be enabled to imitate the voices of little children, of old people, and, in fact, almost every sound which he hears.

Too much attention cannot be bestowed on the *study of sound as it falls on the ear*, and an endeavor to imitate it as it is heard—*for the "secret" of the art is, that as perspective is to the eye so is ventriloquism to the ear*. When we look at a painting of a landscape, some of the objects appear at a distance; but we know that it is only the skill of the artist which has made it appear as the eye has seen it in reality. In exactly the same manner a ventriloquist acts upon and deceives the ear, by *producing sounds* as they are heard from any known distances.

PRACTICAL ILLUSTRATIONS.

NO. I.

THE VOICE IN THE CLOSET

This is the voice in which Mr. Frederic Maccabe, the celebrated mimic and ventriloquist, excels, and the clever manner in which he can adapt it off-hand, as it were, will be best illustrated by the fact mentioned to us by the gentleman in question, whom we call Mr. B. in Mr. Maccabe's presence. Mr. B., who was an invalid, suffering from some nervous disorder, originating by overwork and anxiety, was travelling in Ireland in search of health, and when on his way from Dublin to Cork, he lay exhausted in a corner of a railway-carriage, muffled up in cloaks and wrappers in a paroxysm of pain. At Mallow, two gentlemen entered the carriage, one of whom was in exuberant spirits, and commenced telling some amusing anecdotes. At length the porter came to collect the tickets. They were all handed in but one, when the following colloquy ensued:—

Porter.—A gentleman hasn't given me his ticket.

Gentleman.—Bill, in the next compartment, has the ticket, (tapping at the partition). Haven't you, Bill?

The imaginary Bill, who appeared to be suffering from a severe cold, replied that he had, and the porter would not take it. The official went off to find the ticket, but Bill, in the mean time had vanished. Back came the porter and indignantly demanded the ticket. He was interrupted by a shrill voice in the opposite compartment, crying,—"Porter! porter! why don't you come and take the ticket! There's some one insulting me!" Away went the chivalric porter, to come back puzzled and chafed to receive the ticket, which was handed to him. His hand had not reached the coveted piece of pasteboard, ere the yell of a terrier under the wheels caused the porter to draw back, amid bursts of laughter, during which the ticket was thrown out, and the train moved on. And Mr. Frederic Maccabe stood confessed, but not penitent.

Voice No 1.—To acquire this voice, which we so name for distinction's sake, speak any word or sentence in your own natural tones; then open the mouth and *fix the jaws* fast, as though you were trying to hinder any one from opening them farther or shutting them; draw the tongue back in a ball; speak the same words, and the sound, instead of being formed in the mouth will be formed in the pharynx. Great attention must be paid to holding the jaws rigid. The sound will then be found to imitate a voice heard from the other side of a door when it is closed, or under a floor, or through a wall. To ventriloquize with this voice, let the operator stand with his back to the audience against a door. Give a gentle tap at the door, and call aloud in a natural voice, inquiring "Who is there?" This will have the effect of drawing the attention of the audience to a person supposed to be outside. Then fix the jaw as described, and utter in voice No. 1, any words you please, such as "I want to come in." Ask questions in the natural voice and answer in the other. When you have done this, open the door a little, and hold a conversation with the imaginary person. As the door is now open, it is obvious that the voice must be altered, for a voice will not sound to the ear when a door is open the same as when closed. Therefore the voice must be made to *appear* face to face, or close to the ventriloquist. To do this the voice must not be altered from the *original note* or *pitch*, but be made in another part of the mouth. This is done by closing the lips tight and drawing one corner of the mouth downwards, or towards the ear. Then let the lips open at that corner only, the other part to remain closed. Next breathe, as it were, the words out of the orifice formed. Do not speak distinctly, but expel the breath in short puffs at each word, and as loud as possible. By so doing you will *cause the illusion* in the mind of the listeners, that they hear the same voice which they heard when the door was closed, but which is now heard more distinctly and nearer on account of the door being open. This voice must always be used when the ventriloquist wishes it to appear that the sound comes from some one close at hand, but through an obstacle. The description of voice and dialogue may be varied as in the following examples—

EX. 1. THE SUFFOCATED VICTIM.—This was a favorite illustration of Mr. Love, the polyphonist. A large box or close cupboard is used indiscriminately, as it may be handy. The student will rap or kick the box apparently by accident. The voice will then utter a hoarse and subdued groan, apparently from the box or closet.

STUDENT (*pointing to the box with an air of astonishment*): What is that?

VOICE: I won't do so any more. I am nearly dead.

STUDENT: Who are you? How came you there?

VOICE: I only wanted to see what was going on. Let me out, do.

STUDENT: But I don't know who you are.

VOICE: Oh yes, you do.

STUDENT: Who are you?

VOICE: Your old schoolfellow, Tom, ——. You know me.

STUDENT: Why, he's in Canada.

VOICE (*sharply*): No he ain't, he's here; but be quick.

STUDENT (*opening the lid*): Perhaps he's come by the underground railroad? Hallo!

VOICE (*not so muffled as described in direction*): Now then, give us a hand.

STUDENT (*closing the lid or door sharply*): No, I won't.

VOICE (*as before*): Have pity (*Tom, or Jack, or Mr. ——, as the case may be*), or I shall be choked.

STUDENT: I don't believe you are what you say.

VOICE: Why don't you let me out and see before I am dead?

STUDENT (*opening and shutting the lid or door and varying the voice accordingly*): Dead! not you. When did you leave Canada?

VOICE: Last week. Oh? I am choking.

STUDENT: Shall I let him out? (*opening the door*). There's no one here.

2. THE MILKMAN AT THE DOOR.—This affords a capital opportunity of introducing a beggar, watercress or milkman, and may be varied

accordingly. We will take Skyblue, the milkman; and we would impress on the student, that, although we give these *simple* dialogues, *they are merely intended as illustrations for the modest tyro*, not to be implicitly followed when greater confidence and proficiency are attained.

VOICE: Milk below!

STUDENT: Is it not provoking that a milkman always comes when he is not wanted, and is absent when we are waiting for the cream?

VOICE: (*whistling a bar of "Shoo Fly"*).

STUDENT: Oh, yes, always the broken-hearted milkman as if he was not as happy as a king.

VOICE (*nearer*): Milk below! Why, Sally, where's the can?

STUDENT: Sally will be long in answering, I think.

VOICE: Sally's gadding with the police. Milk below!

STUDENT (*slightly opening the door*): We don't want any milk, my good man.

VOICE: No skim milk for the cat, or cream for tea?

ANOTHER VOICE: Watercresses!

STUDENT: Really, this is too bad. Go away.

VOICE: You owe me ten cents for last week's milk; I was to wait.

STUDENT: This is intolerable. I'll send for the police.

VOICE [*ironically*]: Send for Sally and p'lice, I'll foller.

STUDENT: Impudent rascal.

VOICE: Keep your compliments at home, Master Idlebones.

STUDENT [*opining the door*]: I'll report you to your master.

VOICE [*louder, as the door is opened*]: Will you, young Whippersnapper, pay us the dime, and let us go?

STUDENT offers to pay, while the voice gets weaker in the distance with "Milk below!" until it becomes inaudible.

A conversation may be held in a similar strain with *cellarman*: and, as a rule, the lower notes of the voice will be best for voices in the basement, and formed as low in the chest as possible.

STUDENT: Thomas, are you coming?

VOICE BELOW [*gruffly*]: I should think I was.

STUDENT: We are waiting for the beer.

VOICE [*partly aside*]: The longer you wait, the greater our honor. Mary, have another drop.

STUDENT: Why, the scamp is drinking the beer! Thomas! Who's there with you?

VOICE: Myself. [*Aside*] Make haste with the pot, Mary; he's in such a hurry.

STUDENT: You drinking rascal, how dare you!

VOICE: Coming, sir. The barrel's nearly empty.

STUDENT: I should think so, tippling as you are at it.

VOICE: Now don't be saucy.

STUDENT: The fellow is getting intoxicated. Thomas!

VOICE: Wait till I come. I have waited for you many times.

STUDENT: I suppose it is of no use hurrying you?

VOICE: No, it isn't, my young tippler. I'm COMING! *coming!!* coming!!!

From this illustration the student may proceed to try the second voice.

NO. II.

Voice No. 2.—This is the more easy to be acquired. It is the voice by which all ventriloquists make a supposed person speak from a long distance, or from, or through the ceiling. In the first place, with your back to the audience, *direct their attention* to the ceiling by *pointing to it or by looking intently at it.* Call loudly, and ask some question, as though you believed some person to be concealed there. Make your own voice very distinct, and as near the lips as possible, inasmuch as that will help the illusion. Then in *exactly the same tone and pitch* answer; *but, in order that the same voice may seem to proceed from the point indicated, the words must be formed at the back part of the roof of the mouth.* To do this the lower jaw must be drawn back and held there, the mouth open, which *will cause the palate to be elevated and drawn nearer to the pharynx,* and the sound will be reflected in that cavity, and appear to come from the roof. Too much attention cannot be paid to the manner in which the breath is used in this voice. When speaking to the supposed person, expel the words with a deep, quick breath.

When answering in the imitative manner, the breath must be *held back and expelled very slowly and the voice will come in a subdued and muffled manner,* little above a whisper, but so as to be well distinguished. To cause the supposed voice to come nearer by degrees, call loudly, and say, "I want you down here," or words to that effect. *At the same time make a motion downwards with your hand.* Hold some conversation with the voice and cause it to say, "I am coming," or, "Here I am," each time *indicating the descent with the hand (see examples)*. When the voice is supposed to approach nearer, the sound must alter, to denote the progress of the movement. Therefore let the voice at every supposed step, roll, as it were, by degrees, *from the pharynx more into the cavity of the mouth*, and at each supposed step, *contracting the opening of the mouth*, until the lips are drawn up as if you were whistling. By so doing the cavity of the mouth will be very much enlarged. This will cause the voice to be *obscured, and so appear* to come nearer by degrees. At the same time, care must be taken not to articulate the consonant sounds plainly, as that would cause the disarrangement of the lips and cavity of the mouth; and in all *imitation voices* the consonants must scarcely be articulated at all, *especially if the ventriloquist faces the audience*. For example; suppose the imitative voice is made to say, "Mind what you are doing, you bad boy," it must be spoken as if it were written "'ind 'ot you're doing, you 'ad whoy."[2] This kind of articulation may be practised, by forming the words in the pharynx, and then sending them out of the mouth by sudden expulsions of the breath clean from the lungs at every word. This is most useful in ventriloquism, and to illustrate it we will take *the man on the roof* as an illustration. This is an example almost invariably successful, and is constantly used by skilled professors of the art. As we have before repeatedly intimated, the eyes and attention of the audience must be directed to the *supposed spot* from whence the illusive voice is supposed to proceed.

[2] It is very rarely that a ventriloquist shows a full face to his audience: it is only done when he is at a great distance from them, and is pronouncing the labial sounds, in the manner given, for any movement of the jaws would help to destroy the illusion.

STUDENT: Are you up there, Jem?

VOICE: Hallo! who's that?

STUDENT: It's I! Are you nearly finished?

VOICE: Only three more slates to put on, master.

STUDENT: I want you here, Jem.

VOICE: I am coming directly.

STUDENT: Which way, Jem?

VOICE: Over the roof and down the trap. (Voice is supposed to be moving as the student turns and points with his finger.)

STUDENT: Which way?

VOICE (*nearer*): Through the trap and down the stairs.

STUDENT: How long shall you be?

VOICE: Only a few minutes. I am coming as fast as I can.

The voice now approaches the door, and is taken up by the same tone, but produced as in the first voice. As another illustration, we will introduce the reader to

THE INVISIBLE SWEEP.—This is a striking example of the second voice. Let the student pretend to look up the chimney, and rehearse the following or some similar colloquy:—

STUDENT: Are you up there?

VOICE: Yes. Chimley want sweep?

STUDENT: Really, it is extraordinary. What are you doing?

VOICE: Looking for birds'-nests.

STUDENT: Birds'-nests! There are none there.

VOICE: Dick says there be.

STUDENT: Come down!

VOICE: I shan't.

STUDENT: (*stirring the fire*); I'll make you show yourself.

VOICE: I say, don't; it's so hot.

STUDENT: Come down, then.

VOICE: Don't be so stupid. Let I alone.

STUDENT: Will you come down?

VOICE: Yes, I will.

STUDENT: What's your name?

VOICE (*much nearer*): Sam Lillyvite. I say, what do you want me for among company?

STUDENT: To show yourself,

VOICE (*nearer*): What for?

STUDENT: To let these ladies and gentlemen see that there are many strange things between heaven and earth, but not Sam Lillyvite, the sweep.

Another good illustration is to hold a conversation with a friend who lives on the first floor, and with whom you can converse on any subject—as the *retired and mysterious student*—but the moment the student can master the elementary sounds, he will not need our assistance in providing him with dialogues, which, however simple they may be to read, have *an extraordinary effect when properly spoken.*

POLYPHONIC IMITATIONS.

THE TORMENTING BEE.—It is related that Mr. Love, when young, took great delight in imitating the buzzing of insects and the cries of animals; indeed, it is difficult to decide whether he or Mr. Thurton most excelled in this particular species of mimetic illusion. In all imitations of insect noises, the bee should be heard to hum gently at first, so as in a private party not likely to attract attention till the right pitch is obtained, and be it remembered that the sound, without being particularly loud, can be made to penetrate every corner of a large room. The illusion is greatly increased by pretending to catch the offending and intrusive insect. The humble bee, the wasp, and the bluebottle fly are best to imitate, and afford an agreeable relief to the other exercises of ventriloquial power. To imitate the tormenting bee, the student must use considerable pressure on his chest, as if he was about to groan suddenly, but instead of which, the sound must be confined and prolonged in the throat; the greater the pressure, the higher will be the faint note produced, and which will perfectly resemble the buzzing of the bee or wasp.

Now, to imitate the buzzing of a bluebottle fly, it will be necessary for the sound to be made with the lips instead of the throat; this is done by closing the lips very tight, except at one corner, where a small aperture is left, fill that cheek full of wind, but not the other, then slowly blow or force the wind contained in the cheek out of the aperture: if this is done properly, it will cause a sound exactly like the buzzing of a bluebottle fly. These two instances will show how necessary it is for the ventriloquist to study minutely the different effects of sound upon his hearers in all his exploits. And to make the above properly effective, he should turn his face to a wall; with a handkerchief strike at the pretended bee or fly, at the same time pretend to follow his victim first this way and then that, and finally to "dab" his pocket-handkerchief on the wall as though he had killed it; the sounds should be at times suddenly louder and then softer, which will make it appear as it is heard in different parts of the room.

THE SPECTRE CARPENTER.—The noise caused by planing and sawing wood can also be imitated without much difficulty, and it causes a great deal of amusement. The student must, however, bear in mind that every action must be *imitated* as well as the noise, for the eye assists to delude the ear. We have even seen ventriloquists carry this eye-deception so far as to have a few shavings to scatter as they proceed, and a piece of wood to fall when the sawing is ended. To imitate planing, the student must stand at a table a little distance from the audience, and appear to take hold of a plane and push it forward: the sound as of a plane is made as though you were dwelling on the last part of the word hu*sh*—dwell upon the *sh* a little, as *tsh*, and then clip it short by causing the tongue to close with the palate, then over again. Letters will not convey the peculiar sound of sawing—it must be studied from nature.

A MOUNTAIN ECHO.

Some persons imagine ventriloquism to be an echo; but, as we have said, an echo only repeats what has been said before—it could not answer a question.

An echo is reflected sound, and the reflecting body must be at such a distance that the interval between the perception of the original and reflected sounds may be sufficient to prevent them from being blended together. No reflecting surface will produce a distant echo, unless its distance from the spot where the sound proceeds is at least 56½ feet, because the shortest interval sufficient to render sounds distinctly appreciable by the ear is about one-tenth of a second; therefore, if sounds follow at a shorter interval, they will form a resonance instead of an echo; and the time a sound would take to go and return from a reflecting surface, 56½ feet distance, would be one-tenth of a second.

It would, therefore, be impossible for a ventriloquist to produce an echo in a room of ordinary size, as the walls, being so near, would cause the sounds to be blended, and would only produce one impression on the ear; and yet the skilled ventriloquist can with ease imitate, in a room, a mountain echo. We will give the instructions, as it is very amusing.

Turn your back to the listeners; whistle loud several short, quick notes, just as if you were whistling for a dog; then, as quick as possible, after the last note, and as softly and subdued as possible to be heard, whistle about a third the number of notes, but it must be in *the same note or pitch*; this will cause the last whistle to appear just like an echo at a great distance. This imitation, if well done, never fails to take the listeners by surprise, and causes astonishment. The same thing can be done by shouting. Call aloud any sentence, such as—"Holloa, you there!" Let your voice be formed close to the lips; then quickly, and mind in the *same pitch or note*, speak the same words very subdued and formed at the back of the mouth. This is not difficult, and is very effective.

POINTS TO BE REMEMBERED.

In giving the succeeding instructions, it must be borne in mind that the power and acuteness of hearing is possessed in a greater or less degree by different individuals, and depends upon the sensibility of the auric nerves. It will not be out of place nor uninteresting to show the effect of sound and the manner in which it is heard by the organs of the ear. It is said that the human ear is capable of appreciating as many as twenty-four thousand vibrations in a second, and that the whole range of human hearing, from the lowest note of the organ to the highest known cry of insects, as of the cricket, includes nine octaves.

Sound first strikes the drum or tympanum, a thin membrane which closes the aperture of the ear; when this drum vibrates by the sonorous undulations of the external air; the vibrations are communicated by minute bones, muscles, and fluid in the cavity of the ear, and are then conveyed to the brain; and to show how absolutely necessary it is that all the organs of the would-be ventriloquist should be entire and without fault to succeed well, we will show how the ventriloquist makes that nice distinction of the gradation of sound, and by which he is enabled to judge whether he is causing his voice *to appear* at the proper distance from his audience or not.

Let any one firmly close both ears by stopping them, then speak a few words; now, as the ears are stopped, the sound cannot enter immediately to the drum of the ear, but it takes cognizance of the sound by a passage called the eustachian tube, which extends from the back part of the mouth to the cavity immediately behind the drum of the ear.

The sound vibrations made in the mouth are transmitted along this tube to the interior part of the organs of hearing. Now it is by a nice judgment of sound by this tube that the professional ventriloquist judges the majority of his voices, especially those greatly obscured or muffled. Not only must the auric nerves of the would-be ventriloquist be perfect, but he will become more proficient as he is able to study and understand the human voice. There is the language of emotion, or natural language. When we say natural, we mean the language by which the feelings manifest themselves without previous teaching, and which is recognized and felt without teaching. Some of them are the scream of terror, the shout of joy, the laugh of satisfaction, laugh of sarcasm, ridicule, &c., which are made by man, and understood by fellow-men, whatever may be the speech or country of the other.

There are also distinct qualities of voice, peculiar to each person, both in tone and quality, and the best practice is to try and imitate three or four people's voices, and let them be of a different tone and pitch.

The ordinary compass of the voice is about twelve notes, and a very good practice to the attainment of the art is to call aloud in a certain note, *and then in the octave to that note*; do this several times a day, changing the note, also speak a sentence all in the same note or pitch, properly called intonation, loud at first, and then by degrees lower; this kind of practice will enable the ear to judge of the modulation required to make a voice appear to recede or come near by degrees.

CONCLUDING REMARKS.

When the student is acquainted with the voices before described, he may imitate many others by *contraction and expansion of the glottis, and by modification of the cavity of the pharynx and mouth*. The best way to practice is in a room by himself, to talk loud, and, while so doing, to make all sorts of *contortions with the muscles of the mouth and jaws—first fixing the jaws* in the manner already described, *then drawing the lips inward, next putting them forward, at the same time putting the tongue in different shapes and positions in the mouth*; also by speaking in the natural voice, and answering in the *falsetto pitch*, which is the imitating voice for women and children.

We are confident that enough has been said to enable any one with a good range of voice to attain proficiency in the art; the student always remembering (and it cannot be too often repeated) that *to render a voice perspective, the most essential thing is to attend to the study of sound as it falls upon the ear; then imitate that sound by the different contractions and expansions of the muscles of the throat, mouth, face and jaws*. During these various contractions and expansions, draw in a long breath and talk, first rapidly, then slowly, but always with a *slow expiration of breath*. Do this a dozen times consecutively for several days, at the same time taking particular care to *elevate and depress the roof of the mouth*, especially the back part, as this movement will cause the voice to appear near, or at a distance. Ample directions have been given how all this is done, but let it be understood that it is most essential. The student may then practice before a friend, and he will be astonished to find that he can deceive any listener, as to the point from which the sound comes; and will be gratified that he has become the source of great amusement to himself as well as in the circle in which he moves.

Thus we have acquired a working power in the art which, we trust, we have now explained to the satisfaction of the reader. The progress of the student will, of course, be facilitated by an inherent propensity of mimicry, which often approaches some of the minor attainments of ventriloquism. In every company some person may be found who, without any professional instruction, can give admirable imitations, of the voice, gait, and peculiarities of a friend or acquaintance; thus proving that Nature, to some extent, supplies the basis upon which, if we may use the phrase, the complete superstructure of vocal illusion may be raised. The possession of this quality would amount, comparatively, to little, without instruction and perseverance. Here, as in other respects, practice makes perfect; and, more than that, a diligent application of our rules will invest the originally defective amateur with an attainment which the ignorant will attribute to the possession of a supernatural gift.

All we need say in conclusion is, that the rules propounded will not only clear away imaginary difficulties from the path of the student, but entitle him, like ourselves, to an acquirement more or less near perfection, according to a natural gift of mimicry, and to the zeal with which he may study and practice the art.

THE MAGIC WHISTLE.

It will be pleasant when the wind is howling without, among the snow-laden limbs of the trees, to be reminded of the gay summer by the counterfeit notes of the woodland songsters; or, wandering among the woods and fields in spring or summer time, how glorious to challenge the feathered musicians to a contest of skill with you in their own sweet language. We propose to instruct the reader in the manufacture of a little instrument by which the notes of birds, voices of animals, and various peculiar sounds may be imitated.

First, look at the annexed diagram, and then procure a leek and cut off from the green leaf thereof a piece about the size of the diagram; then lay it on a smooth table, and with the thumb-nail delicately scrape away a small semi-circular patch of the green pulpy substance of the leaf [as represented in the diagram], being careful to leave the fine membrane of outer skin of the leaf uninjured—and there is the instrument complete. It may require several experiments to make the first one, but once having discovered the right way, they are very easily manufactured. The reader may not be aware of the fact that the leaf of the leek has a fine transparent outer skin, which is quite tough, but by breaking and carefully examining one or two leaves, he will soon find out what we allude to.

The way of using this instrument is to place it in the roof of the mouth with the side on which is the membrane downwards; then place it gently in its place with the tongue, and blow between the tongue and the upper teeth. After the first two or three attempts, you will be able to produce a slight sound like a mild grunt; then as you practice it you will find you can prolong and vary the sound somewhat, so that in the course of a couple of days you can imitate the barking of a dog and the neighing of a horse. With two or three weeks' practice, you will be able to imitate some of the song birds; but to produce exact counterfeits of the best singing birds will probably require months of study; the result, however, will reward you for all your pains, for certainly to be able to carry a mocking bird, canary, thrush, cat-bird and sucking-pig in your vest pocket, is no small accomplishment.

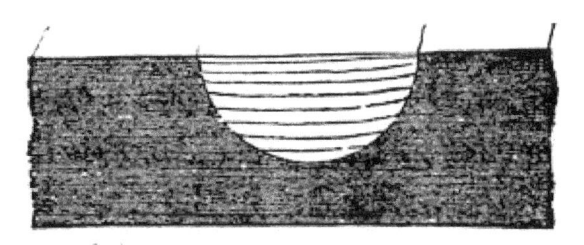

When not using the instrument, it should be kept in a glass of water to prevent its drying.

THE
Hunters' and Trappers'
COMPLETE GUIDE.
A MANUAL OF INSTRUCTION IN THE ART OF HUNTING, TRAPPING AND FISHING.

This book will be found very valuable to those who have not had experience in these healthy, manly and profitable pursuits. The book is thorough in detail in every respect. The young sportsman can learn how to use the Gun or Rifle with ease and precision, and become an unerring shot. The mystery of making, setting and baiting Traps successfully, is shown.

The Best Methods of Catching all kinds of Fish,

Either in the Sea, Lake or River, is told practically and understandingly. The whole

Art of Managing and Training Dogs for Sporting Purposes,

and all about the care of Skins and Furs, so that they will fetch the highest market price, is given, with a vast amount of other valuable information relating to the Hunters Craft.

Milton Keynes UK
Ingram Content Group UK Ltd.
UKHW012314040624
443649UK00007B/625